"God uses people in order to do an amazing work of change in our hearts. The very thing you don't want to have happen is the very thing God wants to do. In *Energy Zappers*, Shaun Blakeney and Wallace Henley share their experiences dealing with difficult people and the biblical principles for turning these energy-draining relationships into character-building ones."

Rick Warren, pastor, Saddleback Church

"Shaun Blakeney and Wallace Henley give clear biblical direction for dealing with the life-draining people we all encounter daily. Their candidness about their own relationships, coupled with practical instructions on the 'Jesus-style' of connecting, makes *Energy Zappers* required reading for anyone in the people business."

Dr. Ed Young, senior pastor,
Second Baptist Church, Houston, Texas

"This book is a great read for anybody who interacts with people. The humor and life experiences caused me to want to jump into the next chapters and keep learning. An easy and informative read!"

Doug Fields, youth pastor, Saddleback Church

"Shaun Blakeney and Wallace Henley understand the emotional price you pay when helping hurting people and, most importantly, what to do about it!"

Ben Young, author, *Out of Control*

"As pastor of a six-thousand-plus church with a worldwide television ministry and a daily radio ministry, my time must be carefully managed. Why am I so weary? In this wonderful book, I have found the answer—twenty-one kinds of people that suck the life force out of me! Here we learn how to handle these brothers and sisters in love without losing our strength. A must read for every leader!"

Dr. Ron Phillips, senior pastor, Abba's House

"We all know that Jesus provides the best example of how we should conduct ourselves when interacting with difficult people, but sometimes that action is easier said than done. *Energy Zappers* addresses exactly how to remain energized by understanding what our priorities are and how to remain focused to achieve them, and also understanding our call to love God and people above all else."

Rebecca Hagelin, vice president of communications
and marketing, The Heritage Foundation

ENERGY ZAPPERS

DEALING WITH PEOPLE WHO DRAIN YOU DRY

SHAUN BLAKENEY AND WALLACE HENLEY

BakerBooks

Grand Rapids, Michigan

Published by Baker Books
a division of Baker Publishing Group
P.O. Box 6287, Grand Rapids, MI 49516-6287
www.bakerbooks.com

Printed in the United States of America

Library of Congress Cataloging-in-Publication Data
Blakeney, Shaun, 1973–
    Energy zappers : dealing with people who drain you dry / Shaun Blakeney and Wallace Henley.
        p. cm.
    Includes bibliographical references.
    ISBN 10: 0-8010-6801-0 (pbk.)
    ISBN 978-0-8010-6801-0 (pbk.)
    1. Interpersonal relations—Religious aspects—Christianity. 2. Conflict management—Religious aspects—Christianity. I. Henley, Wallace. II. Title.
BV4597.52.B565 2007
248.4—dc22   2006034723

Published in association with the literary agency of WordServe Literary Group, Ltd., 10152 S. Knoll Circle, Highlands Ranch, CO 80130.

We dedicate this book to our families,
sources of laughter, joy, peace, refuge, and love

Teresa Blakeney, Austin, and Alyssa

Irene Henley, Lauri, James, Travis,
Mariel, Julia, Jaynie, Joshua, Lucy, and Ciera

CONTENTS

ACKNOWLEDGMENTS

Shaun and I thank our pastors, Rick Warren and Ed Young, for their examples of godly leadership and for the opportunity of serving under and learning from them.

We are grateful to our associates at Saddleback Church and Second Baptist Houston who helped us develop the list of drainers and supplied insights and ideas.

Greg Johnson provided invaluable guidance in nurturing our basic concept to life. Vicki Crumpton and her team at Baker have applied their passion for excellence to make many improvements in the manuscript.

In short, throughout this process, Shaun and I have been surrounded by givers, not drainers, and we are grateful.

Wallace Henley

"I sometimes fancy that every one of the throng that comes to see me daily darts at me with thumb and finger and picks out his piece of my vitality and carries it away."

Abraham Lincoln[1]

"The Son of Man did not come to be served, but to serve, and to give His life a ransom for many."

Jesus of Nazareth[2]

INTRODUCTION

INVASION OF THE DRAINERS

Plug the drain with solid relationships, but know the boundaries.

Drooping nose rings, serpentine tattoos, and mauve-colored spiked hair made the two bewildered boys seem like a nightmare from Dali.

Tobacco odor floated around them, and pewter-colored metal dangled like tiger teeth around their necks. The young men looked like aliens from a black hole. I (Shaun) could almost hear the swoosh threatening to draw in and drain everything orbiting around them.

But I was safe because two of my sturdy youth ministry volunteers clutched the boys' tattooed arms tightly.

"The missions money we were collecting for those starving kids in Africa is missing!" said one of the workers. "We collected seventy dollars, and these two guys were sitting by the money!"

No wonder the Dali models were bewildered. They had no more expected to be in a church service on a Wednesday night than be recruited for the Vienna Boys' Choir. But they had decided, along with some of their pals, to check out the church that was opening its arms to weird people. Now here they were accused of pinching the missions fund.

Madam Outcast

Two thousand years ago, a woman appeared on the cusp of a crowd around Jesus. As far as the elite circling Jesus were concerned, she may as well have had purple hair and a pink mushroom needled into her arm.

For a dozen years, she had been tormented by chronic hemorrhaging. She had to suffer the bite of the physical misery, was stung with being religiously unclean, and had drained her bank account on the medical quackery of her day.

Call her Madam Outcast.

Jesus' reputation as a healer from God had zipped through the region. If she could just touch the dragging edge of his robe, she knew her misery would be over.

Suddenly there was a thin crease in the human wall around Jesus. She wriggled through and, with her fingertips, brushed the fringe of Jesus' garment, down where it slid over the dust.

"Who touched me?" Jesus asked.

The moment Madam Outcast's fingers touched Jesus' hem, he felt that familiar energy pulse launch from his body. It happened every time he touched paralytics and blind people and dead bodies. Jesus knew what had happened. Somebody had received healing, resurrecting, liberating energy, but he had been drained.

Madam Outcast knew too. "I'm the one. I'm the one who touched you!" she blurted out between the sobs of happiness.

"Daughter, your faith has made you well," he said. "Go in peace. You have been healed."[1]

"Don't I know it!" she could have said as she danced off the scene.

I wonder what would have happened that night years ago had we approached the kids from the black hole the way Jesus did Madam Outcast.

Jesus Didn't Dismiss Her but Dealt with Her Problem

Madam Outcast's problem was a bleeding body. Jesus didn't take a detour around Mount Religion. He didn't require that people recite faith formulas; he didn't dismiss Madam Outcast because she was religiously unclean or suffering from poor hygiene. His power went to her need and healed the real problem.

The two kids quaking in the beefy hands of my youth workers were stereotypes of troublemakers. The natural response was to dismiss them as irredeemable, irrecoverable, and irreverent.

But that's not the Jesus-style of connecting. He doesn't dismiss the problem people; he takes care of their real problems. Jesus would have looked beyond spiked hair and metal, beyond tattered robes and haggard faces, to the hidden needs.

Things might have been different that night had my team and I remembered that lesson.

Jesus Delayed His Journey for Her

Jesus was on his way to see the dying daughter of Jairus, a synagogue official, but he skidded to a halt when Madam Outcast touched his robe fringe.

Jesus shows us he's not in the ministry business, but he is in the people business. Sometimes I could wear a sign that says, ATTENTION: DON'T BOTHER ME BECAUSE I'M BUSY TAKING CARE OF PEOPLE. Everything is urgent in the world of ministry. But we should never get so busy with the work that we forget the people the work is all about.

That night when my workers dragged the suspects before me, I was so busy with the details of the outreach service to the outcasts that I forgot about the outcasts!

Jesus Drew Her into the Center

Madam Outcast was unclean and known around town as being religiously impure, so her only hope was to linger at the edge of the crowd, hoping no one would see her.

Outcasts are okay in their place. Have an outreach service tailored for them, but make sure they return to the outer edge when it's over.

But Jesus would have none of this. "Who touched me?" was an invitation right to the center of the circle. Madam Outcast was no longer an outcast but was now called "daughter." Jairus's little girl was more vital to him than his own breath; so Madam Outcast was to Jesus.

Like Madam Outcast, some people live at the edge of the crowd. Perhaps they are rebellious. Or they may think their significance lies at the fringe of the crowd. Many are too shy for the center.

But there are reasons people are rebellious, lack significance, and fear interaction with other people. Connecting Jesus-style means you find out why. The goal is to draw them in.

It saddens me to realize the two "weird" guys had been drawn to the middle of our circle only to be accused of theft!

Jesus Discovered More about Her

Jesus asked, "*Who* touched me?" Not *what*. What he felt could have been a pebble kicked by a stray foot, or the wind.

Jesus wanted to discover the *who*.

Hair and clothing styles, facial characteristics and cosmetics, bangles and chains and jewels, language and speech, gaits and slouches are all *whats*. Somewhere under the *whats* is a *who*. Connecting Jesus-style means you don't stop with the *whats* but keep probing until you find the *who*.

Discovery is done not through programs, plans, and strategies but through relationship. That night my workers and I saw only the *whats*—money was missing, and two guilty-looking characters were nearby.

I Should Have Known Better

Ironically, some people leave the people business because of people.

My dad, one of my heroes, sailed in a big ocean of relationships in his thirty-five years as a pastor. As a kid I watched the ease with which he connected with individuals and thought it must be a lark.

He siphoned his soul, pouring consideration, emotion, and passion into individuals. Dad exhausted his physical strength and resources for the sake of others. He modeled connecting Jesus-style so beautifully that I wanted to walk in his steps.

Somewhere along the way I thudded into the fact that relationships are pricey and painful. I had thought my dad lived in a dreamy world where everybody flocked together like ducks on a summer pond. Actually, he had to work at connecting with people. Some nights he had to get alone with God and replenish his drained inner resources so he could get on with the business of connecting.

The Bible shows relationships are the heart of ministry. But they can sting like a wasp, suck out life like a vacuum, and burn you out like a streaming trail of lava. Relationships are a luxuriant valley on Tuesday, but by Wednesday they can be a barren desert. Yet relationships are the core of ministry, hurtful and costly or not.

The Big Question

Maybe you've asked the question I've posed to myself: *How can I keep on loving and connecting with people without getting so drained I want to quit?* Maybe you've picked up this book while grasping at the last rope to try to keep you from giving up. Could be you've already hammered out your resignation letter and you're dialing your travel agent for a one-way ticket to Tahiti.

Difficult as they are, relationships are unavoidable. Everything in life is based on them. God, parents, spouses, kids, fellow workers, and others compose our daily lives.

Relationships can sicken us but are essential for our health. The aim of this book is to help you flourish in the people business and encourage you to not let people drive you out of it. But I also want to underscore how great the people business can be when we put relationship first.

That's what Jesus did, and it's why we must learn to connect Jesus-style. To do that, we're going to look at specific types of draining people Jesus encountered daily. We're going to try to unlock a mystery: how was Jesus able to deal with the drainers so effectively he was able to bound from one to another with fresh energy?

Jesus Came to Be Drained

Jesus came into the world to be drained. Right up front, he let people know, "The Son of Man did not come to be served, but to serve, and to give His life a ransom for many" (Matt. 20:28).

No serious follower of Jesus Christ can be AWOL when it comes to serving people—even the drainers. But our emotional and physical resources are finite. There must be boundaries, even for Christ's passionate disciples.

God, on the other hand, is infinite. It's a good thing his ability to give, listen, and love is unbounded, because otherwise *we* could be drainers to God! But in his sweeping knowledge of us, he "knows our frame" and "is mindful that we are but dust" (Ps. 103:14).

This is really good news. It means God cuts us slack in dealing with the drainers, even though as committed followers of Jesus Christ our mission is to serve all in the name of our Lord.

Jesus himself laid out boundaries we can follow when he instructed his first disciples in Matthew 10.

Prioritize Your Energy and Other Resources

Jesus' initial command to his disciples was "Do not go in the way of the Gentiles . . . but rather go to the lost sheep of the house of Israel" (Matt. 10:5–6).

The world is full of people without God, but you are a limited human being who cannot touch them all; therefore, prioritize the use of your finite emotional and physical resources.

Bob Pierce was one of the most compassionate men ever to walk the planet, but apparently he missed this important truth. Visiting Korea after the war there, Pierce was touched by the orphans whose parents had died in the conflict. And there were many other countries with hurting children, starving adults, and impoverished masses. Pierce had his own family back in the United States, yet the heartache in the world became his without limits. Bob founded World Vision and spent a good bit of his time suspended thirty thousand feet over an ocean, trying to fly to all the hurting people.

The needs of humanity eventually blurred Bob's sense of proportion. He lost the ability to prioritize—and he lost his family as well.

After his death, Bob's daughter Marilee Pierce Dunker wrote *Days of Glory, Seasons of Night*, detailing the pain of growing up as Bob's child. His emotions were so drained by the masses in the world that he had little left to give his own children. Another of Bob's daughters died by her own hand, Bob's marriage collapsed, and Bob breathed his last breath in lonely solitude.

For good reason, Jesus told his troops to prioritize the expenditure and investment of their energies, and he modeled the principle.

The stony platform around the pool of Bethesda was flooded with pained people hoping for a stirring in the waters, indicating the presence of a healing angel (see John 5:1–9). Jesus walked among them and saw one crippled man he selected from the writhing mass.

Note the prioritization. If Jesus, in his humanity, couldn't touch them all, neither can you. Don't leave your Bethesda, but do allocate your priorities prayerfully and carefully.

Hone Your Focus

A second boundary that will save you from depletion is sharpness of focus. Jesus riveted his followers' minds to a no-nonsense strategy, telling them to announce the nearness of the kingdom of heaven, heal sick people, raise the dead, cure the lepers, and kick out the demons (see Matt. 10:7–8).

There are so many people with staggering need. Where do you start? They need food, clothing, shelter, medicine, and, above all, the message of eternal life.

The key to setting your focus is in knowing who you are. There are many things you can do, but there are jobs that are a perfect match for your gifts and talents.

The Greek philosopher Archilochus wrote, "The fox knows many things, but the hedgehog knows one big thing."[2] The fox darts at the hedgehog with ploy after ploy, but the porcupine-like hedgehog rolls itself up into a thorny ball. "Each day, despite the greater cunning of the fox, the hedgehog always wins."[3]

Be a hedgehog rather than a fox. Reduce the mountain of demand to the hill of opportunity. Whenever possible, select the needs that you are best suited to handle, and set your focus within that boundary.

Don't Fret about Nonessentials

Jesus told his disciples, "Don't think you have to put on a fund-raising campaign before you start. You don't need a lot of equipment. *You* are the equipment, and all you need to keep that going is three meals a day. Travel light" (Matt. 10:9–10 Message, italics added).

Drainers have a way of eating up all you can bring to the table. Then often they want more. There is a point at which you simply can't keep up with the cravings.

When you face the draining people, use what's available to you and don't fret about what you lack.

Stick with Those Who Will Receive You

When you get to your destination, Jesus says to his people, knock on doors and look for a "worthy" person (see Matt. 10:11). Here the term means someone compatible, whose heart is on frequency with your message. And when you find such a man or woman, stick with him or her. You may be surrounded by a whole population, but your service must be to the individual who will take what you offer and use it for others.

In the late 1960s, the buzz was that the successor to Billy Graham would be evangelist John Haggai. The Syrian-descended preacher's star was rising. Millions would read his book *How to Win over Worry*. But suddenly Haggai withdrew from the informal candidacy to be the nation's top evangelist and apparently vanished.

Few people carried a greater burden to reach needy people for Christ than John Haggai. Yet there were so many, and global evangelization was such a huge task. John knew there had to be a different strategy, so he applied literally Jesus' method in Matthew 10. Haggai began to circle the globe. He spent months seeking entry into many nations, looking for leaders who would receive him and his message.

Eventually Haggai planted a training center called the Haggai Institute in Singapore and drew thousands of leaders there.

The students were challenged to go into the provinces and regions of their nations and do for others what John Haggai had done for them: identify the potential leaders and train them to make disciples for Christ.

By 2004, thirty-five years after the launching of Haggai Institute, more than fifty thousand leaders had been trained in one hundred seventy-three nations.[4] John Haggai multiplied himself, Jesus-style, by sticking with those willing to respond.

Move On When Your Efforts Aren't Received

Sadly, some people you want to pour your very heart into simply will not receive you. Jesus says, "If they don't welcome you, quietly withdraw" (Matt. 10:14 Message).

Sometimes you'll be delighted to "shake the dust off your feet," as other Bible translations put it. Often you'll turn away brokenhearted. Yet there are few boundaries for handling drainers more important than this one.

Though you need to discern those who will receive you, it's just as important to recognize those who won't. Jesus practiced this daily. He wouldn't pour himself into Pharisees, but he worked hard ministering to prostitutes and paupers. The Lord wouldn't give as much as a syllable to those who merely wanted to drain him but not receive him.

The Case of the Missing Money

All these years later, I still wonder about the heavy-metal guys accused of ripping off our missions money. Were they drainers or receivers?

Not long after my youth team and I had made the guys from the black hole feel like they were being readied for a firing squad, the case of the missing money was solved. It turned out our financial director had picked up the money and had written a check to the mission for whom we were collecting.

I swallowed my pride and went to visit the spiked-hair kids. It was soon obvious that all we had prayed for and worked for that night went up in a puff of accusation and misjudgment. The kids wanted nothing to do with me, our young people, the youth program, our church, or, worst of all, our God. It was a failure not of *their* stunted morality but of *our* lack of relational skills.

If my team members and I had had the quality of relationship with Christ that should characterize his mature followers, we would have washed those punky kids with grace.

If I had had the right kind of relationship with my youth team leaders, there would have been an overflow of love and grace from them into the young people, including those at the edge of the crowd.

Had I spent more time relating to the fellow who took care of our finances, I would have known exactly where the money was.

Our relational failures pushed those young men deeper into the black hole. What troubles me the most is that it may have cost them eternity itself.

I was so pumped as we went into that special ministry night for the outcasts. But I went home so drained that all I could do was try to cling to the last droplet of my energy. It could have been so different. I could actually have walked away from my brush with the black hole with renewed energy!

So I have returned to the school of relationships. The chancellor, president, dean, and only professor of that school is the greatest leader who ever lived, Jesus Christ.

Great leaders connect, and he connected greater than any. That's why the first relationship a person must develop is the one with the greatest leader.

1

ANGERERS

Angerers drain you by creating discord in your soul and group. When a leader allows angerers to bring him or her to full boil, everybody gets drained. Credibility is cracked, respect ruined, and leadership lost.

Prior to serving at Saddleback Church, I (Shaun) realized the youth ministry I was involved with needed a revolution. We set a purpose-driven concept in the place of our program-centered strategy, and things began to improve dramatically.

Elitist cliques accustomed to running things began to shatter. A parent opposing the changes visited me. The seething dad tried to blunt his fury by repeating, "Now, don't take offense at this . . ." Then came the verbal barbs. I was beginning to take offense anyway.

"Now, *you* don't take offense," I volleyed at one point. "I work for God, not you!" I figured no one could argue with God's strategy. That release of my own frustration solved nothing. The father was even angrier. I had, after all, implied I was hooked into God but he wasn't. My words were intended not to bring reason into the discussion but to deliver a sharp verbal jab.

When the angerers in your midst cause your emotions to redline, allow the truth about your own motives and a focus on your mission to provide a calming effect. Had I done that when the furious father came to see me, I wouldn't have responded to his hostility with my own.

Jeannette[1] was a committed small group leader who also had to make decisions about her responses to a draining angerer. A deep love for God, delight in his Word, and care for people combined to make Jeannette effective. Her flaw was that her compassion meant she was sensitive and edgy when the group didn't go right.

Jeannette regarded Diane as the group's greatest drainer. Diane's attendance was sporadic. She missed meetings, then came in with a big gush, only to disappear again for three or four weeks.

One day Alice, another group member, bumped into Jeannette at the grocery store. "I got a call from Diane the other night," said Alice. "She's saying you didn't go see Amy when she was in the hospital."

Jeannette's heart raced. Amy was hospitalized while Diane was absent from group meetings for three weeks. Diane wasn't around when Jeannette organized meals for Amy's family, picked up her children from school, and did her laundry. Nor had she heard the reports from Jeannette's multiple visits to Amy at the hospital.

Jeannette decided to take the long route home from the store to calm down and think. She realized she had a few options.

React negatively. Jeannette knew she could blister Diane because of her neglect of group meetings. Jeannette marked this option off her list. It would mar her witness and credibility as a leader.

Respond directly. Jeannette considered saying to Diane, "I heard you were concerned about our care for Amy while she was hospitalized. You probably aren't aware of all we did for her. . . ." Jeannette decided not to go with this option. It would too easily become boastful or argumentative.

Love anyway. Jeannette had taught the unconditional love of God. Because Alice knew of Diane's gossip, Jeannette understood other members would be aware as well. This would be a good opportunity for Jeannette to model what she had taught.

Refuse personal offense. Here was the sticking point for Jeannette. She was having a hard time turning loose of the offense prickling her emotions. She knew she had to erect a strong barrier against the riptide of insult inside her.

Rest in God to handle the situation. Jeannette wondered for a moment what it really meant to rest a matter like this in God's hands. Did it mean avoidance and passivity? It actually raised a greater challenge—going forward with a positive relationship with Diane and allowing God to heal her own anger through a constructive engagement with the antagonist.

Concentrate on the people with genuine need. Jeannette knew she could not allow her anger over Diane to divert her from women in the group like Marla, whom she was trying to help walk through a marriage crisis.

Jesus Steadied His Team

First-century Palestine smoldered with anger. Pharisees snarled at Sadducees, who smirked at those they considered their intellectual inferiors. The Romans taunted the Jews, who hated the oppressors. Cheated shoppers loathed the money changers. The rich scorned the poor, who resented the wealthy. The Zealots despised the Herodians, and Herod and his patrons struck cruelly at anyone threatening them.

And everyone was angry at Jesus.

Though Jesus taught his disciples to be lambs, they sometimes wanted to behave like angry tigers. James and John, "Sons of Thunder," rumbled with indignation because a Samaritan village had refused hospitality to Jesus. "Lord, should we order down fire from heaven to burn them up?" asked the incensed brothers (Luke 9:54 NLT).

Jesus shut them up. "You do not know what kind of spirit you are of," he said. "The Son of Man did not come to destroy men's lives, but to save them" (Luke 9:55–56).

Jesus succeeded at his mission, but anger could have derailed it at any point. He demonstrated how important it is for a leader to know the warning signs that the angerer is zapping emotional energy from himself and his followers.

Cracked by Angerers

Angerers can deplete you physically. Allow anger to cook in your psyche, and your body responds with headaches, stomach misery, skin rashes, arthritic pain, nervous twitches, and a host of other symptoms.[2]

The physical strain of anger leaves you limp emotionally. You're too tired to lead, plus you've lost your enthusiasm. Frederick Buechner describes the way anger can drain you.

> Of the seven deadly sins, anger is possibly the most fun. To lick your wounds, to smack your lips over grievances long past, to roll over your tongue the prospect of bitter confrontations still to come, to savor to the last toothsome morsel both the pain you are given and the pain you are giving back—in many ways it is a feast fit for a king. The chief drawback is that what you are wolfing down is yourself. The skeleton at the feast is you.[3]

Knowing the signs would have saved the thirty-five-year career of a man we'll call Pastor Harold. Pastor Harold's valiant service inspired younger men for whom he was a role model. Then anger cracked him.

His last church sparkled with possibilities. But after ten years, Harold began to see that the glimmer was more like polished glass than the glow of a precious diamond. He cultivated people to share his vision only to see others crush the dream and, in some cases, turn his allies against him.

The church of eager anticipation was more a cauldron of seething anger.

Still, Harold pushed forward. The energy required was taxing, but he was committed to the vision. New people came to the church; older members became angry over the newcomers' enthusiasm and left. Then those who had entered with a zeal for growth would become frustrated and, angry at the obstructers, would also exit. This meant the church never grew but barely remained on its precarious plateau.

The angerers fueled Harold's bitterness. Ultimately Harold was mad at God for putting him in a job he hated, and he was mad at the whole church.

Finally Harold and his wife went on vacation. He wanted to get as far away from his local congregation as possible, so the couple traveled to France for a two-week stay.

While Harold and his wife were away, a leader's wife phoned Harold's young adult son. "A few people who don't like your dad have asked the elders to meet and fire him."

Shocked, the young man debated whether or not to tell his father. He concluded if he didn't, his dad would be hurt. So when his father phoned from France, the son told him everything.

"That's it," said Harold. "I've had enough. I'm done."

Pastor Harold resigned from the church and left pastoral ministry altogether, though he and his wife remained as members of the congregation after the angerers left. Years of financial strain ensued, accompanied by job difficulties and frustrations for the entire family.

Harold's anger deepened. Whatever problem he encountered, the church was to blame. The man who had been a gifted teacher and passionate pastor and who had led scores of people into light was now suffocating in darkness. "If I ever see one of those people again, I'm going to punch his face!" he told his son one day.

The emotional energy zappers drained Pastor Harold until his fuel tank was empty. There were some important signs he missed. Recognizing them might have saved him.

It's Time for a Refill

When you perceive the actions as personal insults.

James, a staunch supporter of Pastor Harold, sought to blunt the bullets the angerers were firing at the minister.

James had strong gifts of discernment and administration. He recognized mistakes that made Harold a target for the angerers. James assumed he had Harold's complete trust and offered suggestions about how his friend could respond more effectively to the angerers.

But rather than taking James's recommendations positively, Harold took them as personal insults. He lumped in James with those seeking his destruction. A vital relationship was lost.

Anger had so blurred Pastor Harold's vision that he couldn't make out his friends from his foes.

When personal insults are allowed to fester.

There's a point when you must decide to turn away from personal insults. To cling to them is the equivalent of fertilizing a garden. Whatever you feed grows.

For years, Pastor Harold ignored the antagonists. He tried to develop tough skin. Pastor Harold crashed when he became so weary under fire that he no longer exercised the discipline of refusing to focus on the anger aimed at him.

Even positive criticism was then regarded as a personal insult. Played over and over, the words festered in his mind.

When you are diverted from your identity and mission.

Paul wrote, "Walk in a manner worthy of the calling with which you have been called, with all humility and gentleness, with patience, showing tolerance for one another in love, being diligent to preserve the unity of the Spirit in the bond of peace" (Eph. 4:1–3).

Threatening to "punch" his angerers was hardly compatible with Pastor Harold's identity and mission. His identity was in Christ, who was silent in the torrent of accusation and abuse hurled by the angerers as he was on trial before Pilate and Caiaphas. Pastor Harold might have understood that his emotional energy tank was approaching empty had he noted how much he was veering from his identity in Christ.

Further, Pastor Harold's calling was a shepherd, not a thrasher. Had he grasped the contradiction of a shepherd wanting to harm his sheep, he would have been appalled at how drained he was.

When you begin using your emotional energy to plot against the angerers.

Pastor Harold's remark about punching his angerers was more a quip than a threat. Sadly, though, there are leaders whose creative zest turns to sinister daydreams.

Psychologist Pauline Wallin reminds us,

Plotting revenge may not be such a good idea. . . . Sure, you're more rational this way, but while you're plotting, you are investing time and energy into something that may not be worth it in the end. Your inner brat is still prominent, making mountains out of molehills. The plotting keeps your anger alive and active.[4]

Dealing with Angerers

Connect with Who You Are

If you are settled about your identity, the barbs of the angerers won't threaten you with self-doubt.
Jesus said,

> The servant is not greater than his lord. If they have persecuted me, they will also persecute you; if they have kept my saying, they will keep yours also. But all these things will they do unto you for my name's sake, because they know not him that sent me.
>
> John 15:20–21 KJV

Affirming identity in Christ means recognizing angry responses as part of the package. Angerers will always oppose the genuine follower of Christ because darkness is antagonistic to Christ, the Light of the world.

This is why when James and John wanted to nuke the Samaritan villages, Jesus told them, "You do not know what kind of spirit you are of." Jesus encouraged them to remember their real identity.

Connect with What You're About

"The Son of Man did not come to destroy men's lives, but to save them," Jesus reminded James and John. Jesus showed that if you are clear about your mission, the angerers will hardly be noticed.

Jesus never lost sight of why he was in the world. Because of that, the antagonism was actually a confirmation that he was on track.

Connect with Your Own Limitations

Honesty about yourself will douse the angerers' darts. Jesus' urging that James and John take a hard look at the type of spirit motivating their anger is an exhortation for everybody.

Paul counsels people to "be angry, and yet do not sin; do not let the sun go down on your anger, and do not give the devil an opportunity" (Eph. 4:26–27).

Every individual has a "besetting sin" (see Heb. 12:1 KJV) to which he or she is particularly vulnerable. For some, that sin is anger. The powers of darkness are able to build a thick-walled fortress on that hefty ground. It's vital to recognize your limitations. Doing so will set you free from the tendencies that allow your adversary to make a fool of you and your mission.

Connect with Your Responsibility

Rather than agreeing with the Sons of Thunder about the Samaritans, Jesus wanted the brothers to understand *they* were responsible for what they allowed the Samaritans' anger to do to them.

The angerers have no power over you if you don't let them. To douse the angerers, don't be a victim who blames them for your loss of temper; take responsibility for your actions.

Sometimes you must get away from the angerers so contemplation can replace consternation. Resignation is not the answer, but refreshment is. Soak your emotions in quiet reflection, away from the fury.

Pastor Harold's burns healed as mulling the wrongs done him by the angerers was replaced by musings on his identity in Christ. Rather than running, Harold remained in the church, and friends helped him find new strength.

The good news is that Harold's story doesn't end with his angry departure from the church and ministry. Ultimately he shook off his self-imposed victimization, and recovery began.

His wife bumped into the spouse of one of those Harold had wanted to punch in the face. She told Harold's wife that her husband had been diagnosed with cancer and had only a short time to live. Sometime later the couple came to church. When Harold and his old foe spotted each other, their eyes locked. The angerer was gaunt, skeletal, gray-skinned, and hairless. Harold's true identity welled up within him, propelling him toward the man who had inflicted so much pain on him and his family.

Rather than delivering a punch, he embraced his antagonist. That act, carried out before the watching eyes of the church, signaled forgiveness more than words could express. The flood of God-given compassion doused Harold's anger and enabled him to love the angerer.

As I write, it has been ten years since that moment. Pastor Harold has been on a positive track of growth and recovery ever since. Like Job, his latter years will be the greatest, most fruitful of all.

I (Shaun) know because Pastor Harold is my dad.

2

CHATTERERS

The chatterer zaps you and your group of emotional energy by always talking and rarely listening.

Your group is at the moment of breakthrough. Crises are at the threshold of resolution. Vision is about to be grasped, confusion cleared up, and personal concerns settled.

You recognize and appropriate time for parentheses—moments of silence to let the discoveries and realizations sink in. Everyone in the room is quiet. Except Charlie Chatterer. Mindless words shatter the moment. You try to figure out how to recapture the magic.

But it's too late. Charlie has pulled the plug. You and the team members are drained of emotional energy.

Jesus and Lady Chatterer

"Give me a drink," says Jesus to a Samaritan woman he encounters at a well (see John 4).

Rather than dipping the bucket, Lady Chatterer wants to talk protocol and political correctness. "You're a Jew and I'm a Samaritan woman. Why are you even talking to me?"

She moves on to other topics. Jesus offers her Living Water, and she wants to discuss the dipper. He seeks to show her she's having an encounter with God in human flesh, and she wants to talk history. He brings her prophetic truth, and she wants to chitchat about theology and which "mountain" is the right one for worship.

Her gabbing is gobbling away the most important conversation of her life, and she's turning the conversation into a monologue.

"Go and get your husband," Jesus tells her (John 4:16 NLT).

"I don't have a husband," she sputters.

"You're right! You don't have a husband—for you have had five husbands, and you aren't even married to the man you're living with now" (John 4:17–18 NLT).

The lady is hushed. Recovering, she says, "You must be a prophet." Now her tongue begins to rattle again, and she launches off on the religious differences between Jews and Samaritans.

Patiently Jesus unfolds the truth to her, culminating in astonishing news: "I am the Messiah." Lady Chatterer is speechless. She sprints back to her village and tells everyone about the man she's met. The whole population streams out to him.

Jesus had dealt successfully with the lady whose penchant for chatter had caused her to spend her life as a drainer.

Jesus was effective with the chatterer because he kept bringing her back to the point. He used every rabbit trail to lead to the main road of truth. Finally he routed her to the blockbuster—the revelation of himself as Messiah.

It's Time for a Refill

When you feel like you're trying to hold a sailboat on course in a typhoon.

Your group, along with its mission and tasks, is the sailboat. The typhoon is the gale of hot air sweeping the space around you. You heave to, trying to bring the team back into focus, restore vision, and get everyone back on the compass heading to your goal.

But the effort becomes so exhausting you're ready to quit and turn the rudder over to someone else. All you want to do is find a quiet place below deck away from the deluge, stuff cotton in your ears, and sleep.

When your own passion is being doused in a torrent of words.

I (Wallace) was a young reporter at the *Birmingham News* during the civil rights battle. Some in leadership realized it was time for a new era. An energetic, visionary mayor was elected. Like Winston Churchill in World War II England, his initial speeches ignited people all over the city to rebuild race relations and the town's reputation.

But the mayor—unlike Churchill—was a chatterer more than an orator. After a while, his brilliance became blah-blah, and inspiration faded into enervation. One day the *News'* city editor marked through a reporter's story on yet another speech by Birmingham's chief executive, saying, "He would be a great mayor if he didn't talk us to death!"

Dealing with Chatterers

Listen to What the Chatterer Is Really Saying

I (Shaun) took some of our ministry volunteers to a leadership conference in Atlanta. I looked forward to bonding as well as learning.

Two of my associates—call them Barney and Brutus—
were chatterers. Barney was from New York and Brutus
from New Jersey. Riding from the airport, they debated
the qualities of the two states regarding everything from
buffalo wings to sports teams.

Everyone laughed nervously as the two magpies
cawed at each other. But as the days wore on, our group
noticed the arguing and felt the struggle. I had hoped we
would be inspired by the conference and return home
with new energy. Instead, Barney and Brutus were draining us all.

Ironically, the problem sizzled to its boiling point during
a session on how to handle difficult people.

Barney raised his hand. I shuddered as the conference
leader gave him the floor. "How do you deal with a person
who talks your head off?" Barney had the gall to ask.

Before the conference leader could reply, Brutus answered, "Just listen to a tape recording of yourself and
figure out what to do with *you*!"

The session on how to handle difficult people got ugly.
A standoff was developing. I pulled Barney and Brutus
outside.

"Guys, you have really humiliated yourselves," I said.
"Worse, you have embarrassed God, our leaders, and our
church. You two have got to relax!"

Then the real issue emerged. Both men had deep-seated
feelings of rejection. Barney was afraid people would like
Brutus more than him. He tried to top every story Brutus
told. Brutus despised himself and compensated by spouting
opinions he thought would make him look smart.

Jealousy was the fuse that set off these talking bombs.
As Barney and Brutus realized what was happening, they
listened to each other with eager, open hearts to learn how
their pain could be healed and their behavior changed.

Similarly, the reason the woman at the well can't pull Jesus
off topic is that he's listening to the real concern cloaked

in her chatter. She feels guilty, spiritually dry, and deeply rejected.

Jesus turns every verbal volley she shoots at him into a question or provocative comment exposing her core anguish. He plunges deep into her soul, touching the desert of her heart.

Lovingly Confront the Chatterer with the Truth Being Evaded

Jesus gracefully silences the chattering woman with three straight, unequivocal statements.

"I will give you water that will quench your thirst forever." The Samaritan woman's lifestyle is a dead giveaway to her arid desperation. She thirsts for unconditional love. All the chatter about water and religion and political correctness is a cover for her real need. Jesus slices through it, straight to her cracked heart. He waits until the time is right and uses the woman's own words to help her confront the reality about herself.

Jesus has high sensitivity to the rhythm of the conversation. He himself is not a chatterer. He knows when to speak and when to be silent. Career counselor Marty Nemko says, "Unless you're saying something you know deserves more than a minute, at the 30-second mark, look for a place to stop. If your listener wants more, he or she can ask a question."[1] It was that style that helped silence the chattering woman. Her questions and responses deepened with each exchange with Jesus until she listened and heard.

"You have had five husbands, and the man you're living with now is not your husband." Chatterers almost always try to veil the brutal facts about their behaviors. Wordy folk are able to contrive elaborate webs of verbiage to hide behind.

I (Wallace) made this discovery as an aide in the Nixon White House. Once, while crossing the country on Air Force One, the president made a comment to reporters that seriously misconstrued facts known to almost everyone. The gaff became evident before the presidential airplane landed. Knowing he would be faced by herds of carnivorous journalists, Nixon had his pilot circle the destination airport until his wordsmiths crafted a statement that would cover the president's mistake.

Chatterers try to do endless cycles around the landing field of reality. Their words are the engines, and their hot air is the fuel keeping them aloft, away from the hard, unyielding strip of truth.

People who really care about others will tell them the truth. Jesus sees that the woman at the well is about out of fuel herself. She has drained herself in the process of draining others. Jesus hushes her chatter long enough to bring her down to land on truth—which is the only way she can truly soar.

"God is Spirit, and those who worship Him must worship Him in spirit and in truth." The chattering lady wants to divert her encounter with truth by arguing religion. The Samaritan sages worship God over at Mount Gerizim, she notes, while the Jews look to Mount Zion in Jerusalem. She asks, "So why do you Jews think Jerusalem is the only place to worship?"

Chatterers love arguing and talking around an issue, and religion is one of their favorite topics. Without insulting her, Jesus signals she is too preoccupied with religious trappings and is missing the essence.

The wise leader, like Jesus, refuses to be drawn into the debate. He or she chooses the right moment and words to cut through and land on the truth.

Dr. Bill Bright, founder of Campus Crusade for Christ, had this ability. Many years ago, I (Wallace) sat in a hotel room with Dr. Bright, who listened patiently as I chatted nonstop about politics, ministry, the state of contemporary theology, and a host of other topics. In his characteristic style, Bill nodded quietly, occasionally inserting a comment.

Suddenly he looked at me and asked me if I had truly yielded my life to the lordship of Jesus Christ. I sputtered.

The chatterer was silenced. I realized I sat in the presence of a man who had forsaken all to carry out Christ's call. For the next hour, my attention was riveted as Dr. Bright taught me from his studies and experience what it meant to walk under Christ's control. That moment launched a redefining process within me that changed the direction of my life. But to get there I had to close my mouth and listen.

A new category of humanity has emerged in the twenty-first century: the "chattering class," people whose lives—and sometimes livelihoods—are based on chatter.

Bruce Walker says the chattering class has now deteriorated into the stammering class.[2] When the chatterers no longer have anything substantive to say, they blather on, fading into a mere stammer. As the shallowness of contemporary culture proves, chatterers drain whole societies dry.

Effective leaders deal positively with these emotional energy zappers. As Jesus shows—and the Samaritan woman would testify—the drain of the chatterers can be turned into life-transforming gain!

3

CLINGERS

Calvin Clinger holds on to you so tightly he constricts your movement, and he wears you out as you try to carry him everywhere.

At times you feel like the Ancient Mariner. In Samuel Taylor Coleridge's epic poem, the old sailor kills an albatross, a pious bird of good omen, and when the weather gets nasty, his crewmen assume it's because the Mariner killed the animal, which they chain around his neck.

Every leader has times he or she feels choked by a clinger.

Calvin Becomes a Clinger

Calvin asked Barry, his team leader, to work with him in improving his ability to communicate. Barry taught Calvin how to outline, illustrate, and hang sentences together. After four months, Calvin was crawling out of his cocoon and seemed on the way to becoming a better communicator. Barry decided to let the butterfly soar.

"I want you as the speaker for the conference we're planning," Barry told him. "This will give you the opportunity to put into practice everything I've taught you. I want you to assemble the speech using the principles we've discussed. After the conference, we'll have a critique session."

Calvin agreed. Barry had been expected to speak for the event, but his schedule was jammed, and he didn't have time to prepare. Now Calvin had taken the load off his back.

Or so Barry assumed. Actually, rather than turning Calvin into a communicator, Barry had created a clinger.

The next morning Calvin tapped on Barry's office door. "I need just a little bit of help getting started with my outline," he said. And on it went daily. Usually the sessions ate up Barry's morning.

On the night Calvin spoke, Barry realized *he* had actually written the message. Later that night Barry told his wife, "I didn't teach Calvin anything except how to get somebody else to write his speech."

Calvin displayed the number one characteristic of the clinger: he became a load rather than a load bearer.

Jesus and the Clingers

Jesus' experience revealed two types of clingers: the positive (the students) and the negative (the stalkers). He shows us how to deal with each.

Carry the Positive Clingers Until They Can Carry Themselves

The positive clingers were the people who really wanted to learn from Jesus. One group of positive clingers hung on to Jesus because they shared his mission and wanted to be part of it. Take, for example, the group of women who followed him all over the country.

[Jesus] began going around from one city and village to another, proclaiming and preaching the kingdom of God. The twelve were with Him, and also some women who had been healed of evil spirits and sicknesses: Mary who was called Magdalene, from whom seven demons had gone out, and Joanna the wife of Chuza, Herod's steward, and Susanna, and many others who were contributing to their support out of their private means.

Luke 8:1–3

Many of the women—like Mary Magdalene—had significant need yet were in a culture where women had to stand at the edge of the crowd. Later Mary Magdalene and others of these women were the first bold enough to go out to Jesus' tomb.

The disciples might have tried to protect Jesus from his women "clingers" as they sought to shield him from parents begging help for their children. But he said, "Let the children alone, and do not hinder them from coming to Me, for the kingdom of heaven belongs to such as these" (Matt. 19:14).

There were many "positive clingers" who fell into the "such as these" category, like the blind man whose eyes Jesus opened. "Immediately he regained his sight and began following Him on the road" (Mark 10:52).

All of these people were spiritual, emotional, mental, and sometimes physical basket cases. But Jesus carried them because he saw the possibility in them. He knew they wanted to walk, not cling. His joy was in seeing them stand on their own and begin to make their first tentative, shaky steps.

In some ways they may have been like a child I'll call Sabrina. Joe, a member of the church I (Wallace) served as pastor, begged me to come to his home and pray for his five-year-old daughter, who had been born with seriously deformed legs. She could not walk; she had to drag herself through the house.

Week after week I visited her home. Her parents and I agreed on a goal: we would press on until Sabrina could stand on crutches and walk to me down the long aisle of our church sanctuary. Her "homework" between my visits was to practice standing on her crutches, an agonizing feat for the child.

Eventually her mother called. "We're ready!" she said.

I met Sabrina and her mom at the church auditorium. I went to the front end of the rectangular sanctuary. Sabrina's mother positioned the child at the other end, almost one hundred feet away. The child began to hobble toward me and finally collapsed in my arms, laughing over her achievement. I thought, *This is what Jesus intended for the church—that it be a place where all the clingers learn to stand and walk for themselves!*

There were positive clingers in Jesus' day who were considering walking with Jesus but wanted to check him out first. "Many even of the rulers" (John 12:42) believed in Jesus, though they wouldn't go public for fear of being booted out of the religious elite. They too followed from afar.

Nicodemus was an exception. A Pharisee, a member of the Sanhedrin (the high religious court), and one of the richest men in Jerusalem, Nicodemus clung to Jesus until he saw truth one night.

Joseph of Arimathea was another positive clinger. He was a secret disciple of Jesus "for fear of the Jews" (John 19:38). He didn't come out into the open until that afternoon when he took the body of Jesus from the cross and placed it in his own tomb.

Jesus' objective was to bring the positive clingers to the point where they could carry themselves. He showed the difference between loosing the clingers and cutting the clingers loose. The former means helping positive clingers to become load bearers rather than loads. The latter refers to severing relationships with negative clingers before they become a drain. The ideal always is to transform negative clingers into positive, committed followers.

Cut the Negative Clingers Loose before They Drain Everyone

Another group of clingers was the stalkers. These negative clingers were like the sign seekers who shadowed Jesus. Their motives were many, including curiosity and the desire to confound Jesus by testing him. But Jesus confronted the negative clingers:

> One day some teachers of religious law and Pharisees came to Jesus and said, "Teacher, we want you to show us a miraculous sign to prove that you are from God." But Jesus replied, "Only an evil, faithless generation would ask for a miraculous sign; but the only sign I will give them is the sign of the prophet Jonah. For as Jonah was in the belly of the great fish for three days and three nights, so I, the Son of Man, will be in the heart of the earth for three days and three nights. The people of Nineveh will rise up against this generation on judgment day and condemn it, because they repented at the preaching of Jonah. And now someone greater than Jonah is here—and you refuse to repent. The queen of Sheba will also rise up against this generation on judgment day and condemn it, because she came from a distant land to hear the wisdom of Solomon. And now someone greater than Solomon is here—and you refuse to listen to him."
>
> Matthew 12:38–42 NLT

Jesus had come to reach everyone with the Good News. The sign seekers would have been welcome in God's kingdom had they been willing to respond with faith. Because they wouldn't, Jesus had to cut them loose and move on.

Help Negative Clingers Face the Truth about Themselves

Jesus told the negative clingers they were part of a "faithless generation" because they weren't thinking for themselves but were simply aping the worldview of their culture.

Every church and organization will have negative clingers. Negative clingers are "camp followers," people who follow a military unit to its various encampments. Sometimes their purpose is exploitation. During the American Revolutionary War, for example, camp followers were often prostitutes.

Similarly, negative clingers linger at the edge, motivated by curiosity or the desire to find a flaw they can exploit. They don't share the beliefs, values, or mission of the church or organization they stalk but are motivated by a contradictory worldview. They need to be confronted with that truth and given an opportunity to get in or get out.

Give the Negative Clingers What They Need

Jesus gave the scribes and Pharisees hovering at the edge of his "camp" the sign *he* chose, not the variety they sought.

The sign seekers wanted a sensational demonstration to prove Jesus' messiahship. Jesus gave those signs to positive clingers such as the woman with chronic bleeding, the Roman soldier whose servant was sick, the synagogue official whose daughter had died, and many others. But Jesus wouldn't compromise with negative clingers or allow them to frame the debate. The statement about Jonah may have seemed mysterious to them, but it showed there was a truth they knew nothing about.

The sign the stalkers needed was truth, and that's what Jesus gave them. The hard truth is a sharp knife. It will either sever the negative clingers from you or remove their conniving motives. Give them the truth and they will either leave you or join you.

Show Negative Clingers Where Their Behavior Will Lead

Negative clingers need the brutal facts. Jesus told the scribes and Pharisees trying to trap him that their attitude would lead to condemnation or captivity, or both.

The clingers' stalking spirit will translate to other facets of their lives. Repeated actions become habitual behaviors that become lifestyles. Negative clingers risk becoming people who never can be counted on to leave the periphery and get their hands dirty—and sometimes bloody—with the rest of the team.

"Fish or cut bait" is the stark choice for the negative clinger. At some point, bold leaders must put it that bluntly.

I (Shaun) know the joy of seeing a negative clinger become a committed follower willing to "fish." A young woman we'll call Rhonda came to work for me as an intern. She had the potential to be a really great minister to young people, but she was undermotivated. I would be talking to our leadership team, and Rhonda would be circling the room, talking on her cell phone. I would give Rhonda an assignment, and she would always leave loose ends that got everybody tangled.

We conducted many fun events for the teens, and Rhonda could always be counted on to be present. Yet when it came to service projects and teaching activities, Rhonda was either mentally and emotionally distant or physically not present at all.

Rhonda clung to us, but she seemed unwilling to become a load bearer.

Finally I had to loose this clinger or cut her loose. As we approached Christmas break, I explained the way others perceived her behavior and how it was draining the group. "You have a choice," I told Rhonda. "If you can't change your attitude and work ethic, then you can just stay home when you go there for Christmas break!"

It was one of the hardest conversations I'd had because of my love for Rhonda. But the outcome was one of the most joyous of my career. Rhonda did a lot of reflecting while she was home for the holidays. When she returned, it was with a renewed attitude and a readiness for action. She was no longer a clinger but was a committed member of our team—a load bearer rather than a load.

It's Time for a Refill

When the clinger gets heavy even though he's your "brother."

For Rachel, it was a "sister" who became an albatross. Rachel was just beginning what she anticipated would be a long career as a Christian counselor. Nan was her first case. Pastor Willis had asked Rachel to try to help Nan, whose husband, Gerald, was a key lay leader.

A year later, the last thing Rachel wanted to be was a Christian counselor. Weekly for a year, Nan had come to Rachel's office with the same stories of woe from her past, the same misery of the moment, and the same anxieties about the future. After twelve months, Nan was still the same mass of misery as when she and Rachel had begun. It occurred to Rachel that Nan enjoyed talking about her travails and really didn't desire healing. In the process, Nan had zapped almost all Rachel's emotional energy.

Dealing with Clingers

Recognize It's Best to Loose Them

Jesus sought to bring his disciples to a high level of strength, maturity, and responsibility so they could keep walking when he was no longer around to carry them. Therefore, it was in the best interest of the clingers to learn to stand on their own two feet.

Sometimes a leader has to face the fact he or she is enabling others to be clingers. When that happens, the leader is more focused on his or her interests than that of the clinger.

Some leaders, for example, are micromanagers. They force an employee to be a clinger by looking constantly over the worker's back. Such managers are driven by two fears: jealousy (they fear the employee will perform better than they do) and anxiety (they fear the employee will fail and make them look bad).

Jesus had no such fears. He called in his team, which then included seventy-two people, paired them up, and sent them into towns he would soon visit. He unwrapped their clinging arms from his neck and gave them the hard truth: "I am sending you out as lambs among wolves" (Luke 10:3 NLT).

There's a time for information, but what must follow inevitably is perspiration. This means showing people how to handle situations, take responsibility, and carry out what they've been taught; otherwise the leader hasn't done his or her job.

Set Clear and Impenetrable Boundaries

Jesus shared his expectations with the seventy-two he sent out.

> Don't take along any money, or a traveler's bag, or even an extra pair of sandals. And don't stop to greet anyone on the road.
> Whenever you enter a home, give it your blessing. If those who live there are worthy, the blessing will stand; if they are not, the blessing will return to you. When you enter a town, don't move around from home to home. Stay in one place, eating and drinking what they provide you. Don't hesitate to accept hospitality, because those who work deserve their pay.

If a town welcomes you, eat whatever is set before you and heal the sick. As you heal them, say, "The Kingdom of God is near you now."

Luke 10:4–9 NLT

The team members were clear on what to do and what not to do. They would have to figure out how to eat and get lodging, since Jesus told them to take no money. And nowhere did Jesus tell them to run back to him for a loan before the mission was done.

Leaders loose clingers when they set boundaries the clinger is not permitted to cross. A major reason Nan remained a clinger in counseling was because Rachel didn't set boundaries in the form of expectations.

Turn the Clingers into Load Bearers

For three years, Jesus headed his followers toward a strategic moment. It arrived forty days after his resurrection. They followed him out to the Mount of Olives. Earlier he had told them, "It is to your advantage that I go away; for if I do not go away, the Helper will not come to you; but if I go, I will send Him to you" (John 16:7). Now the time for his departure had come.

Three years earlier, all those now standing with Jesus on the mount had been clingers. Slowly and patiently, Jesus had transformed them into load bearers. Just before he ascended, Jesus told his team, "You will receive power when the Holy Spirit has come upon you; and you shall be My witnesses both in Jerusalem, and in all Judea and Samaria, and even to the remotest part of the earth" (Acts 1:8).

The clingers were loosed to take responsibility for the mission. The drain was turned to gain!

4

CONFUSERS

Confusers lack clarity about mission, method, motive, and other factors essential to a team's success, and they infect everybody with their blurred vision.

Take the case of a young woman I (Shaun) call "Connie Confuser." If I explained to Connie that everyone in the group was to study the same material, which had already been prepared, she would happily say, "I understand." Then she would write her own curriculum.

If I gave Connie a detailed instruction on how class time was to be formatted, she'd cheerily say, "Got it!" But I'd be left to sort things out when she devised her own format.

If I wanted a class, Connie would convert it into a huggy cluster. If our plan called for small group, highly interpersonal time, Connie would switch to a lecture format that bored almost everyone.

Connie threatened to put our whole organization into the critical care unit. Connie's group had no more connection with our mission and purpose than a honeybee with a helicopter. The result was that I was drained, the volunteers began to lose their focus, and we wondered what had happened to our joint goals and plans.

"I am so sorry," Connie would say every time we met. "Now I know exactly what you're talking about." But there was no hint in her actions that her confusion bug had been zapped.

Jesus and the Confusers

Jesus was surrounded by confusion and confusers. One Sabbath, at the synagogue in Capernaum, he told a crowd, "I am the living bread that came down out of heaven; if anyone eats of this bread, he will live forever; and the bread also which I will give for the life of the world is My flesh" (John 6:51).

Immediately the confused bunch buzzed with arguments and questions. "How can this man give us his flesh to eat?" they asked one another. Some of those who had signed on with Jesus abandoned him over his remarks.

> After this, Jesus stayed in Galilee, going from village to village. He wanted to stay out of Judea where the Jewish leaders were plotting his death. But soon it was time for the Festival of Shelters, and Jesus' brothers urged him to go to Judea for the celebration. "Go where your followers can see your miracles!" they scoffed. "You can't become a public figure if you hide like this! If you can do such wonderful things, prove it to the world!" For even his brothers didn't believe in him.
>
> John 7:1–5 NLT

People Were Confused about Jesus' Mission

Jesus' whole mission was about serving others. He loved to be called "Son of Man," signifying his identity with flawed human beings. Jesus' followers knew he had submitted to John's baptism of repentance, marking the fact that though he had no sin, he was on the side of those who did. They even heard him say he had come not to be served but to serve. Still they didn't get it—not even on that night when he washed their feet (see John 13:5–11).

The confusers in your midst hear you, yet they don't hear. Jesus had the religious leaders in mind when he said,

> I speak to them in parables; because while seeing they do not see, and while hearing they do not hear, nor do they understand. In their case the prophecy of Isaiah is being fulfilled, which says, "You will keep on hearing, but will not understand; you will keep on seeing, but will not perceive; for the heart of this people has become dull, with their ears they scarcely hear, and they have closed their eyes, otherwise they would see with their eyes, hear with their ears, and understand with their heart and return, and I would heal them."
>
> Matthew 13:13–15

Abraham Lincoln's "team"—his Cabinet—was full of confusers who didn't hear Lincoln's heart and consequently were befuddled regarding his mission. The situation was so bad Attorney General Edward Bates wrote in his diary that Lincoln's was "not an administration but the separate and disjoined action of seven independent officers, each one ignorant of what his colleagues are doing."[1]

The confusers drain you and your team of the vital unity required to reach a goal and achieve a mission. To correct the misperceptions, it's vital for a leader to keep the mission and its goals before the team constantly and in a variety of ways.

People Were Confused about Jesus' Method

The majority was against the adulterous woman that day when the Pharisees dragged her to Jesus. Jesus shocked everyone—including his closest associates—by forgiving her. How could a man preaching purity let a harlot off the hook? Jesus' method wasn't theirs.

Nor was it when Jesus went over to Lazarus's house for a visit. Mary fetched costly perfume and lavished Jesus' feet with it. Judas pouted, "That perfume was worth a small fortune. It should have been sold and the money given to the poor" (John 12:5 NLT). Judas and everyone in hearing range were dumbfounded when Jesus said, "Leave her alone because she's anointing me for burial. You'll always have the poor with you, but I won't be around much longer" (vv. 7–8, authors' paraphrase).

And there was the time Jesus spat on the ground, made mud, and rubbed it in a blind man's eyes (see John 9:6).

Stunning methodologies. Confusing conclusions.

Jesus could see the cross looming before him, and his methods were geared to that larger vista. Those whose range of vision was narrower thought his strategies peculiar, and they confused others with their limited grasp of the situation.

As Jesus shows, those confused about methods must be brought into close relationship with the leader. Trust and commitment develop, even though team members may still be unclear about the methods.

People Were Confused about Jesus' Motive

"I am the Light of the world," Jesus declared (John 8:12). "You are making false claims about yourself!" replied the indignant Pharisees (v. 13 NLT). The legalists were sure Jesus' motive was to be a religious huckster.

Like his Lord, John Wesley's motives regarding his "method" and aims were widely misunderstood. Confusers surrounded him, insisting Wesley wanted to destroy Anglicanism—the traditional church in England—and launch his own movement.

Actually, John Wesley believed there should be a return to "primitive Christianity" as seen in the New Testament church. But he wanted to restore the Anglican Church to that historical model, not leave the church or start a competing movement.

Confusers throw themselves off track when they take their eyes off the leader's heart. Jesus shows that group members who know the character of their leader will trust his or her motives, even if they don't understand the leader's actions.

People Were Confused about Jesus' "Moment"

The disciples snored away in the world's pivotal moment as Jesus agonized in the Garden of Gethsemane. Three times he sought to rouse them. The third time, Jesus told them, "*The hour has come*; behold, the Son of Man is being betrayed into the hands of sinners" (Mark 14:41, italics added).

At other points in his life, Jesus had to remind the people around him the "hour" had *not* yet come. At the Cana wedding, Jesus had to caution even his mother, who wanted him to do a miracle to solve the crisis of depleted wine: "Woman, what does that have to do with us? My hour has not yet come" (John 2:4).

Because Jesus was clear on his mission, method, and motive, he also understood the appropriate timing—the moment—when he was to reveal himself as Messiah. Confusers, however, became impatient, wanting to precipitate the "moment" thoughtlessly without attention to the whole purpose of their organization.

Jesus would allow no one to determine his "moment." Though his followers didn't always grasp why Jesus would not do more to go public, their close walk with him brought them confidence that he knew when to do the works marking him as Messiah.

Types of Confusers

The Muddled

The muddled are hapless folk confused about everything. They mean no harm; they honestly don't get it. The muddled are invariably muddlers, infecting others with their confusion.

Billy Joe operated the sound system at his church. When he managed the audio for high school events, he cranked the volume to extremes. At first the youth pastor was convinced Billy Joe planned to wreck the church's youth ministry. Ultimately though, the youth pastor got to know Billy Joe's motives.

Billy Joe had grown up in the hard-rock scene. He remembered the concerts of his youth—when nuking sound systems were first being refined—and how he had enjoyed the pounding of percussion and bass. Billy Joe assumed if megadecibels attracted him to concerts in the old days, they would bring in the young people to his church.

He was muddled but not malicious.

The Malicious

The muddled may be innocent, but the malicious are out to defeat you. They understand your mission, methods, motives, and moment, and they sow confusion about your organization and its purpose intentionally.

Often what drives the malicious confusers is jealousy and rebellion. Confusion was the favorite strategy the Pharisees used in their attempts to discredit Jesus. Through trick questions, they sought to befuddle Jesus and make him look foolish in front of people. Their frustration mounted as Jesus answered with insight that amazed everyone. Insight doesn't always top malicious attitudes, however.

I (Shaun) once served a church suffering an internal split personality. The church as a whole was growing, but parts of its ministries seemed unchanging. My assignment was to focus on a vital facet of the body whose growth was stunted.

Confusion became the weapon of choice of those resisting the changes. They gathered a group secretly and planted ideas that threatened to undermine the credibility of the church's leadership, including mine.

Ultimately I confronted the confusers: "I was chosen to lead this ministry, and you'll have to trust me." That didn't end their efforts to sow confusion, but it did alert the other members of the group that I intended to carry out my mandate from the church's senior leadership.

The Mischievous

The mischievous confusers, like the muddled, are not bad-intentioned. However, for them every project is a plaything, every task a toy. They love to see how "creative" they can be, and they wind up bending and pounding your plans until you no longer recognize them.

The Modifier

The modifier believes he or she can improve on your plans and introduces confusion by constantly tweaking things to a "better" way.

Jason, a staff member at a large church, encountered a modifier when he headed up a True Love Waits conference for teens in the congregation. He knew he needed to enlist Janet, another member of the church staff, who was loaded with talent.

"You can be the program director or the conference speaker," Jason told Janet. "The choice is yours." Janet's early life had been characterized by promiscuity, but Christ had transformed her. She opted to be the event speaker.

Two weeks later Jason was billed for programming items purchased by Janet but not relevant to the plans developed by Tricia, the program director. Not wanting to offend, Tricia and her team tried to work in the materials Janet had ordered, but there was no fit. Jason and Tricia tried to get a refund on the items Janet had ordered. "Remember, Janet, you're not in charge of programming. You chose to be the speaker," Jason reminded her. She nodded in agreement.

The confusion Janet spread was draining the conference planners of their vision and enthusiasm. Jason knew there was no malicious intent behind Janet's efforts. She was a modifier who believed she could come up with a better plan. Instead she confused everyone.

It's Time for a Refill

When you begin to doubt your own mission and strategy.

Hardly any human endeavor shows this as graphically as parenting. There are so many voices promoting so many child-rearing theories that many moms and dads have lost confidence in their abilities to care for their offspring.

There's good reason parents get confused. "The Century of the Child" was the tag given by a writer in the 1900s. "What began as the Century of the Child," writes Marilyn Gardner, "ended as the Century of the Expert." Over a mere twenty-five years, "the number of parenting books has increased fivefold."[2]

Parents are leaders with a mission, and when those in charge get confused, it spreads to those looking to them for guidance. Psychoanalyst Bruno Bettelheim lamented that confused parents rear confused kids.[3]

Solomon describes this draining force of ideas, theories, concepts, philosophies, strategies, methods, and plans:

> I said to myself, "Look, I am wiser than any of the kings who ruled in Jerusalem before me. I have greater wisdom

and knowledge than any of them." So I worked hard to distinguish wisdom from foolishness. But now I realize that even this was like chasing the wind. For the greater my wisdom, the greater my grief. To increase knowledge only increases sorrow.

Ecclesiastes 1:16–18 NLT

Dealing with Confusers

Be Clear on Who You Are

Peter Sellers was the hapless Inspector Clouseau in the *Pink Panther* series. But Sellers played many other parts in his life. In fact, one day he was approached by a fan who asked, "Are you Peter Sellers?" Sellers shot back, "Not today."[4]

Your appreciation for who you are may lag on gray days, but never lose the sense of who you are. When you know your identity, others know it as well. It's hard for the confusers to mislead you and your followers when your identity is established clearly and consistently.

Be Clear on Your Mission and Its "Moment"

John describes Jesus' journey to Jerusalem to attend the Feast of Tabernacles. At first, his relatives—not yet believers—pressed him to go at a certain time.

> "Go where your followers can see your miracles!" they scoffed. "You can't become a public figure if you hide like this! If you can do such wonderful things, prove it to the world!" . . .

> Jesus replied, "Now is not the right time for me to go. But you can go anytime, and it will make no difference. The world can't hate you, but it does hate me because I accuse it of sin and evil. You go on. I am not yet ready to go to

this festival, because my time has not yet come." So Jesus remained in Galilee.

John 7:3–4, 6–9 NLT

Jesus was able to stand firm because he was clear about his mission and its timing. Because of that clarity, Jesus didn't succumb to the confusion that characterized his human relatives.

Be Clear on the Confusers and Their Agenda

The confusers were hard at work when Jesus arrived in Jerusalem for the Feast. John reports, "There was much grumbling among the crowds concerning Him; some were saying, 'He is a good man'; others were saying, 'No, on the contrary, He leads the people astray'" (John 7:12).

Among the confusers were opinionated people who thought they knew the Scriptures but were really in the dark. Jesus couldn't be the Messiah, they said. "We know where this man is from; but whenever the Christ may come, no one knows where He is from" (v. 27).

Yet Micah the prophet declared God's Chosen One—the Christ—would come from Bethlehem. Some confusers will be those folk who misquote Scripture as a reason for believing and acting as they do.

None of this fazed Jesus, because "he knew what people were really like. No one needed to tell him about human nature" (John 2:24–25 NLT).

Jesus knew who the confusers were and was neither surprised nor shaken when they tried to lasso him and his followers.

Stay Your Course

Peter himself unwittingly tries to insert confusion at one of the most critical moments in Jesus' ministry. Once again, the issue revolves around a decision about going to Jerusalem. This time Jesus is determined to go to the city because the time is right. Jesus tells them bluntly that his enemies will capture and crucify him, but he will rise from the dead.

"God forbid it, Lord! This shall never happen to You," Peter blurts (Matt. 16:22). But Jesus knows what he must do and refuses to be pulled off his course, even by his closest associate.

Jesus demonstrates that leaders who know themselves and their mission cannot be diverted from its course and accomplishment. Instead, they clarify the confusers through their commitment and determination.

5

CRITICS

"Unplug the machine!"

At first I (Shaun) thought Matt was the incarnation of caustic criticism.

"You're looking more at programs than people," Matt said. "You're all about schedules and logistics. *Unplug the machine!*"

There are times God sends us prophets. We don't recognize them until we rub the fuzz off our hearts, lower our defenses, and try to hear their passion. Matt was telling me we were allowing a church ministry to become an insensitive, grinding machine that cranked out plans and programs but sometimes forgot people.

"Unplug the machine!" became the official motto of our ministry. A man we could have brushed off as a mean-spirited critic was used of God to give our vision a much-needed lift.

Two Kinds of Critics

Sadly, there are critics out to do nothing more than drain you. They heave their complaints on your head to get them off their own shoulders. Such critics have no goal other than transferring their misery and meanness to you.

Then there are critics like Matt. They believe in you and bring constructive criticism to help you reach your goals.

Richard Clarke played that role in my (Shaun) life. God used him and my father to shape my destiny. Richard was the youth leader in our church. For six of my formative adolescent years, he was my friend and a voice of unyielding truth.

One way to differentiate between the positive and negative critics is whether they approach you with an air hammer or a chisel. One type of critic wants only to shatter you, while the other aims to shape you. Skillfully Richard wielded a chisel against the hard marble of my stubbornness, and God used him to equip me for the work I do today.

Richard taught me to turn confrontation into a positive opportunity to build relationship. "You win people to what you win people *with*," he told me. For example, my tendency was to place priority on getting people to events. They often wound up committed to the event rather than to other persons—namely, Jesus Christ. Richard thus critiqued my mind-set and strategies as a sculptor, not a demolisher.

Another way to cull the negative critics from the positive truth tellers is to consider what we might call the Jeremiah principle. In calling Jeremiah to his prophetic work, the Lord tells him, "I have appointed you this day over the nations and over the kingdoms, to pluck up and to break down, to destroy and to overthrow, to build and to plant" (Jer. 1:10).

The negative critics leave out the last command, "to build and to plant." The constructive critics hear and practice the entire command.

For me (Wallace), that critic was an unlikely and unsuspecting "prophet." Lula Connell was the living definition of an eccentric. She had taught Russian in college, cultivated reluctant musicians, ate tins of sardines for lunch, and probably wrestled alligators. But by the time I knew her, she was in her sixties, and she was our church secretary.

As my high school days approached, my single-parent mother fretted about where I would get lunch money. So Pastor Williams hired me to work in the church office on Saturdays—not a pleasant chore for a fourteen-year-old boy.

Mrs. Connell printed the Sunday bulletin on Saturdays. She cranked up a mimeograph machine, the ink flew, and 1,400 sheets of paper whirred out the other side, imprinted with the story of our church for that weekend.

I was fascinated—until that inevitable moment that came every Saturday. "Look at that splotch of ink on the covers," Mrs. Connell would say in her gravelly voice. "That won't do. You haven't done it right. Erase the ink mark from all 1,400 copies!"

I would squint to see a little blemish the size of a gnat, then get angry. It was five p.m., and I wanted to go home.

It wasn't until I was an adult that I understood. Mrs. Connell knew I was paid by the hour, and she was determined to keep me working as long as possible so my pay for that day would pile up. But along the way, that dear critic helped develop in me a passion to get the job done all the way and get it done right.

The caustic critics want to snuff out your passion, but the constructive critics play the prophetic role that can propel you to your best. It's vital you sort them out so the mean-spirited ones can't drain you and the positive critics can build you.

Jesus and the Critics

Hebrews 12:3 says, "Consider Him who has endured such hostility by sinners against Himself, so that you will not grow weary and lose heart." There's plenty to consider when one thinks of Jesus and the critics. They were all around him constantly, threatening to drain him.

But note that the Scripture speaks of him *"enduring* such hostility."* Jesus faced the bitterest of critics day after day yet kept pressing on. The Bible's Greek word for *endure* means to be under a heavy load but to refuse to let it crush you. The Jesus who bore the cross through Jerusalem's streets first carried the cumbersome load of the critics throughout his world.

The Scripture says "consider" him so we won't crack under the strain of the critics. We must think about Christ rather than the critics. That's not a mere religious response but an action that sets us up for a positive outcome when we're cut by criticism.

Further, says Hebrews, if we do this, we won't "grow weary and lose heart." These words describe the draining effect of criticism. It can wear us out and sap us of all enthusiasm. We must put our minds on a positive setting—and that course leads us straight to Christ, even against gales of criticism.

People who sail the North Atlantic have observed a strange phenomenon: icebergs often tend to move opposite strong gales. The wind may be from the north, but the berg plows on northward. The reason is the bulk below the water is caught in currents far beneath the surface and persists in riding those surges rather than the surface winds.

Jesus kept moving in the deep currents of his purpose—despite the tempest of criticism up at the surface—because of his depth, his profound relationship to the Father, and his commitment to his mission.

It's Time for a Refill

When every critic seems to be an opponent.

"You're all against me!" shouted Percy Paranoid to Ralph, Percy's top assistant. The accusation caused Ralph to wince.

He knew his motives, and he had always tried to give his boss truth so Percy wouldn't be destroyed.

But there were so many critics around Percy he decided everyone was the enemy, including Ralph.

When you indulge the sycophants and avoid the critics.

It seemed the only people Percy wanted near were those whose vocabulary was "Yes!"; "How high do you want me to jump?"; and "How wonderful you are!"

When you want to lop off the heads of people who tell you the truth.

Percy was so drained he had fallen into the Herod syndrome.

> [King] Herod himself had sent and had John arrested and bound in prison on account of Herodias, the wife of his brother Philip, because he had married her. For John had been saying to Herod, "It is not lawful for you to have your brother's wife."
>
> John 6:17–18

Herod eventually had John the Baptist's head chopped off at the request of Herodias's daughter. Herod was happy to accommodate her to save his skin.

Ralph noticed Percy was firing more and more people. The problem was they were the folk who could have saved his skin because they told him the truth.

Dealing with Critics

Recognize the Critic Type and His or Her Need

People who benefit from critics work at discerning the character and motives of their detractors. Rather than being reactive, smart leaders identify the negative critics and seek to understand and minister to their needs.

Ramona was a small group leader who eventually discovered this truth. From day one, fellow group member Andrea was a nuisance. She nettled Ramona at every turn. Ramona's style was stifling or loose, the group meetings were too long or too short, and the program materials were too cumbersome or too shallow.

One day Ramona and Andrea wound up in the same prayer circle at a group meeting. Saundra, another woman, was asking prayer for her father, who was gravely ill. Unexpectedly Andrea began to weep. Saundra's mention of her dad brought to mind the pain Andrea's abusive father had brought her.

Suddenly Ramona understood that Andrea's experience with her father, an authority figure, made her distrustful of anyone in an authoritative position. Ramona recognized that because she was a leader, Andrea felt threatened around her. Ramona decided to become a friend to Andrea. Ultimately Andrea became a trusted ally, making many contributions to the team.

Astute leaders count the positive critics as the prophetic voices bringing them much-needed truth. Wise leaders know the critics may be sounding an alarm that could keep them from disaster. You can turn the drain of criticism into gain by touching the needs of your negative critics and respecting the positive critics as trusted allies who have the courage to tell you the truth.

Let Criticism Spur You to Positive Action

Sam Walton, founder of Wal-Mart, valued critics. He advised managers, "Listen to everyone in your company. . . . To push responsibility down in your organization, and to force good ideas to bubble up within it, you must listen to what your associates are trying to tell you."[1]

Critics who said we would never fly helped motivate Orville and Wilbur Wright to keep tinkering in their bicycle shop until they were in the sky.

The prickly darts of criticism from the Pope helped drive Michelangelo to hoist himself up on a high scaffold in the Sistine Chapel and paint for endless hours until its ceiling was a masterpiece.

The critics spurred Abraham Lincoln into the White House. They cawed about his appearance, his roots, his poor education, and his previous failures, but Lincoln kept standing and walking until he became leader of his nation and liberator of slaves.

Make criticism your ally, not your adversary. Until you are perfect, you need the critics to show you the subtle flaws that can crack your whole dream. Don't write off the critics, even the caustic ones.

Get Your Emotions out of It

Confederate general Robert E. Lee reportedly was asked his opinion of an officer who had criticized him frequently and publicly. Lee gave a glowing report of the soldier. When reminded of how the officer had criticized him, Lee responded, "You did not ask his opinion of me, but my opinion of him."[2]

Critics can irritate you only to the extent you allow. A person secure in Christ can either route hurtful words from the mind to the emotions or end-run the emotions. For the latter, the negative criticism can be sent right into the human spirit, which is indwelt by the Holy Spirit. For example, rather than mulling over a barb in the mind until the sting is felt in the emotions, it's better to send it to the spirit, where it bumps into several questions.

What does the love of Jesus say about my critic? The eighteenth-century English evangelist George Whitefield understood this principle. He had many critics, some of whom would send him caustic letters. In response to a particularly vicious note, Whitefield replied,

> I thank you heartily for your letter. As for what you and my other enemies are saying against me, I know worse things about myself than you will ever say about me. With love in Christ, George Whitefield.[3]

What does the joy of Jesus say about my feelings toward the negative comments? Joy is not an emotion but a state of being centered in the regenerated spirit. Critics can rob us of happiness only when we forget to tap into the well of Christ's joy within us. The critics nailed Jesus to the cross, which he endured "for the joy set before Him" (Heb. 12:2). They could snatch everything but his joy.

What does the peace of Jesus say about the criticism? By its very nature, criticism stirs a tempest in your soul. One definition of *peace* is "harmony." The adversary's aim is to fragment people so that body, soul, and spirit are fighting one another. But the person who "coheres" as a whole being in Christ doesn't fly apart under criticism. The spirit ministers calmness to the soul, which influences the body to settle down.

What does the patience of Jesus say about my attitude toward the critics? According to a legend, Abraham spotted an old man struggling toward him and went out to meet him. He washed the traveler's feet and gave him food and drink.

"Don't you worship God?" Abraham asked when the old man didn't pray before eating. "I worship fire only, and reverence no other god," the man replied.

Indignant, Abraham asked the weary traveler to leave. Later God asked Abraham where the visitor was. "I forced him out because he did not worship you," Abraham answered. God replied, "I have suffered him these eighty years although he dishonors me. Could you not endure him one night?"

The story is legend, but the principle stands. The God who indwells us is absolutely patient. We should draw on that reserve when the critics enter our tent.

What does the kindness of Jesus say about my response to my critics? Kindness, in the New Testament Greek, combines the ideas of moral excellence with a gracious attitude and desire to be helpful. People who want to respond to critics with Christlikeness don't "kill" them with kindness but *bless* them with kindness.

Alexander Maclaren, the nineteenth-century Scottish-born preacher, knew the bite of criticism. He was involved in the denominational clashes of his day. "Kindness makes a person attractive," he said. "If you would win the world, melt it, do not hammer it."[4]

What does goodness say about the way I need to handle this situation? Goodness signifies a generosity of spirit. Responding to critics with this attitude means being generous in understanding them but also being generous with truth. Jesus was "good" in his gentle responses to Martha's criticism for "being late" to help Lazarus. But he was equally "good" when he gave sharp truth to his caustic critics, the scribes and Pharisees.

What does faithfulness say about how I need to continue to stand in the onslaught of criticism? The leader hit with criticism doesn't fold if he or she is responding in the Spirit of Christ. Rather, faithfulness is the steel spine enabling a leader to stand, even under withering assault.

A college psychology professor unwittingly helped me (Wallace) understand the importance of faithfulness. He suggested the "preacher boys" in his class wanted to be in the pulpit because they had a high need for acceptance and recognition. I evaluated his claim in relation to my own life and concluded it was probably true. *So what do I do about it?* I asked myself. *Do I quit because my motives may not be 100 percent pure?* I concluded that on my own I would probably give up. But God's faithful Spirit refused to let me throw in the towel. That was more than forty years ago.

What does gentleness say about my total demeanor when I am stung by critics? The New Testament term *gentleness* denotes a wild, energetic stallion well-harnessed and under control. Many a leader has made a fool of himself and destroyed his credibility by throwing a temper fit aimed at his critics. But if we allow the Holy Spirit to bridle our responses to our critics, we can respond with strength that is tempered and tamed.

What does self-control say when I am tempted to strike back at my critics? Self-governance is vital in everything from organizations to nations. Edmund Burke said people can have liberty in proportion to their willingness to chain their own passions. Puppies need leashes, but disciplined animals can run free because they understand where the boundaries are. Similarly, leaders must evidence self-control, especially in the face of criticism.

These nine questions are all based on the fruit of the Spirit listed in Galatians 5:22–23. The man or woman whose spirit is alive with God's Spirit can choose to respond positively to criticism.

Get Your Mind and Ears into It

Management expert Danny Cox says,

> People who are unhappy will tend to *find fault* in anything, everything, and everybody. When morale is high, even mistakes are not dwelled upon in an orgy of negative thinking. When morale is low, even the greatest victories might be picked apart and talked down.[5]

Getting your mind and ears into the criticism may alert you to the need for a morale boost within your organization.

Be Proactive

"Who do men say that I am?" Jesus asked his followers one day (see Matt. 16:13). The Lord was providing opportunity for his team to surface their thoughts. Wise leaders allow unspoken concerns and opinions to be vented in an environment where they can respond and provide clarification.

Author Anthony D'Souza says it's important for followers—even the critics—to have a forum in which they can be heard, and that leaders should

- make the forum safe and comfortable for followers to be heard;
- accept the data gracefully;
- not become defensive or hostile;
- show acceptance and appreciation;
- attempt to make use of the data.[6]

Ask the Critic for a Solution

My (Wallace) old friend Joe McKeever recalled how evangelist Dwight L. Moody was criticized for his evangelistic methods. On one occasion, Moody decided to press a critic for a better way and asked the man how he did evangelism. "I don't," the critic replied. "In that case," said Moody, "I prefer the way I do it to the way you don't."[7]

Put the critic in charge or on the spot. Highlight the fact it's easy to point out the problem, but it's a far greater challenge to provide a solution.

The apostle Peter said we shouldn't be returning "evil for evil or insult for insult, but giving a blessing instead; for you were called for the very purpose that you might inherit a blessing" (1 Peter 3:9). Such a response will "heap burning coals" (see Rom. 12:20) on the head of the detractor.

That truly confounds the critics!

6

CYNICS

Among your critics will be cynics, those who drain you of faith and confidence by hurling disbelief, mockery, and rancor at you.

Cynics almost drove me (Shaun) from the ministry just as I began. The youth band players at a church I served became more focused on performance than godly lives. Sid was a key member of the music group but was drifting seriously from the Lord.

"I'm pulling you out of the band," I had to tell Sid one day. He stared back in disbelief. "Sid, you're a leader," I continued. "Kids will follow you. You can get back in the band and help lead worship again when your life matches the message in your music."

Sid's parents were livid and left the church. Two months later, they phoned the senior pastor. "We want to come back to the church and reconcile with Shaun," said Sid's dad.

My pastor and I visited Sid's home. Everyone seemed nervous. The youngsters were scooted upstairs, and the adults sat down at a table for coffee and conversation.

"Why did you take our son out of worship leadership?" Sid's father asked.

"It's not a permanent change," I answered. "I want to see some spiritual growth in his life before he starts leading praise again."

"How can you help anybody grow spiritually?" the dad growled back. "No one respects you!"

I turned to the senior pastor. "I gave them the benefit of the doubt, and they haven't kept their end of the bargain. I thought we were here for reconciliation!"

My pastor came to my defense and said to Sid's parents, "I'm very disappointed in you. I feel lied to because you told us you wanted to make amends."

With that, the pastor and I got up from the table and left the house.

That night I planned the statement I was going to make to the pastor, lay leaders, volunteers, and youth as to why I was leaving the church and ministry. My swan song was going to be something like this:

> I'm not quitting because I'm mad but because I'm a failure. I've tried for two years to turn things around in the area to which you assigned me, but I've done nothing but frustrate people. I cannot continue in a role in which I stir up turmoil in people's hearts. I quit!

I never delivered my departure speech. Deep inside, I felt the Holy Spirit tugging at me to hang in there. I realized I had bought into the allegation of the cynics that no one respected me. I was letting their acid eat away at my self-respect, confidence, and belief in my call. As I wrestled with the matter in prayer, I sensed if I didn't give up God would use the cynics to help me grow. Not only did Sid need spiritual development; I did too.

Cynic Population Grows

Cynicism has become a feature of popular culture. Organizational psychologists say almost half of all American workers are cynical about their companies.[1] In 1992, researchers found that the "value" of cynicism was among eight of the core values of twentysomethings.[2]

That generation apparently carried forward its "core values." Author William Strauss says, "Cynicism and the absence of heroes has reached a 'settled acceptance.'"[3] The cynic's outlook on life is that "selfishness and guile" are at "the base of human nature."[4] Some people withdraw into cynicism as a means of coping with a shaky world. Cynics especially are distrustful of management and leadership.

The attitude spills over into churches and their programs and ministries. Pastors and other leaders need to know how to recognize and deal with the cynics who populate their pews.

Some will be like a man who, in a conversation with me (Shaun), excused his cynicism like this: "I always tell the truth, no matter how it hurts. I'm *brutally* honest; that's just the way I am."

The man revealed more about himself than he intended. He showed cynics don't care whether their critiques are heard and acted upon for positive improvement. They're self-focused and want to say whatever is on their minds. He was right: cynics commit acts of verbal brutality.

In identifying the cynics, it's important to distinguish between cynicism and skepticism. Skeptics are doubters while cynics are despairers. Skeptics are open to change, but many cynics don't believe there are positive options to be embraced. Skepticism is a "healthy response"[5] to a world that often overpromises and underdelivers, but cynicism is a less wholesome approach. And invariably draining.

Jesus and the Cynics

Jesus swam in a sea of cynicism, and the tempest rose to a Category 5 hurricane when he was hanging on the cross.

The scorn was in full surround sound. It echoed from the hillsides around Golgotha and bounded up to his ears from the people below the cross. And who knows what the powers of darkness were hissing at him?

The mob taunted, "You who are going to destroy the temple and rebuild it in three days, save Yourself! If You are the Son of God, come down from the cross" (Matt. 27:40).

The religious elite joined in with their cynical mockery, using the spoken word against the Living Word.

> He saved others; He cannot save Himself. He is the King of Israel; let Him now come down from the cross, and we will believe in Him. He trusts in God; let God rescue Him now, if He delights in Him; for He said, "I am the Son of God."
>
> verses 42–43

Perhaps the most biting voices pounding at Jesus that day came from the horizontal level. "The robbers who had been crucified with Him were also insulting Him with the same words" (v. 44). One of them hollered, "Are You not the Christ? Save Yourself and us!" (Luke 23:39).

But there's been a subtle shift with Jesus' other partner in pain. Luke, the historian, records it like this:

> But the other answered, and rebuking him said, "Do you not even fear God, since you are under the same sentence of condemnation? And we indeed are suffering justly, for we are receiving what we deserve for our deeds; but this man has done nothing wrong." And he was saying, "Jesus,

remember me when You come in Your kingdom!" And He said to him, "Truly I say to you, today you shall be with Me in Paradise."

Luke 23:40–43

Somehow, despite his own torment, the observant thief was able to see beyond himself. He watched how Jesus handled the cynics. Perhaps what the thief saw firsthand was what Peter would remember years later, when he wrote, "He did not retaliate when he was insulted. When he suffered, he did not threaten to get even. He left his case in the hands of God, who always judges fairly" (1 Peter 2:23 NLT).

No words exploded from Jesus to blast the cynics. The thief was persuaded away from his cynicism by Jesus' actions in the acid bath of sarcasm.

It's Time for a Refill

When you're tempted to join your own opposition.

That night at Sid's parents' house, if a vote had been taken on whether or not I (Shaun) should stay in the ministry, I would have voted against myself.

When you're losing confidence in your ability to accomplish your mission.

Some managers focus on belittling the employee and his or her abilities, while others buttress a worker's self-confidence and ability to reach goals. Two bosses in my (Wallace) forty-year work experience stand out as examples, one negative and one positive. In the Nixon White House, I was close to the bottom of the chain of command, Bob Haldeman at the top. Haldeman's style sapped a person's confidence in his or her ability to get the job done.

At the other end of the spectrum is Ed Young, senior pastor at Second Baptist Church of Houston, where I am now one of the pastors. Young is direct but always focuses on helping his team members grow in their skills.

Among Ed Young's goals is that of developing young men and women as leaders. At this writing, Second Baptist has five campuses. The booming West Campus, for instance, has a weekly attendance of over seven thousand. Each campus has a team leader, and Young mentors each team leader. He points out areas of needed improvement in administrative or communication skills but shows his confidence by releasing important assignments to the leaders.

When the cynics cause you to begin to doubt your mission.

The drain of the cynics has reached near-bottom when their caustic remarks begin robbing you of passion for your mission.

Judas was the top cynic among Jesus' disciples. He illustrates how one can devolve from skepticism to cynicism. When Judas questioned the economy of pouring precious oil on Jesus' feet, it may have been the quandary of the honest skeptic. But when he coldly and cravenly sold out Jesus for thirty pieces of silver, it was the deed of a soured human being.

Judas's plunge into cynicism culminated in his doubting and abandoning Jesus' mission of seeking and saving the lost and offering his life as a ransom for many. Judas wanted a mere revolutionary to overthrow a political and military oppressor, while Jesus' mission covered the whole of the human race and spanned eternity.

When you begin to doubt the mission, the cynic sulking either in your own heart or at the edge of your group is draining you to the point of empty. A crash soon will follow.

Dealing with Cynics

It's about Lifestyle, Not Verbal Arguments

Live before and with the cynics in such a way as to persuade them. In the words of the old spiritual, when Jesus stood before cynical Pilate and caustic Caiaphas, he "never said a mumblin' word." What carried the day ultimately was Jesus' irrefutable lifestyle. People might have made cynical comments about his actions, but his character couldn't be called into question, though there were many who tried.

Skeptics may be won over by argument and debate. Forget it with the cynics. They have already made up their minds, and no amount of intellectual fisticuffs will change them.

Let Your Actions Win the Debate

For one thing, the positive actions you carry out in the face of cynicism will benefit you. Management expert Rosabeth Moss Kanter says confidence comes "from experiencing your strengths in action."[6] But the impact of your positive actions in the pit of cynicism is much broader than that.

Jesus faced such cynicism when he stood before Pontius Pilate, who had played the game of Rome to climb the political ladder. Pilate had placated the pompous, flattered the fawning, and compromised whatever principles he had. His heart was encrusted with the cold cynicism of a Roman military professional who would just as soon lop off someone's head as look at him or her. As the bureaucrat in charge of Palestine, he had seen all the religious fraud the region produced as its most abundant crop.

Now Jesus of Nazareth stood before him.

Pilate gave Jesus every opportunity to make sweeping claims and defend his innocence. Instead, Jesus looked up at Pilate and, with blood streaking his face, his wrists bound, and a mob of jeering people around him, undertook no defense.

Finally Pilate called for a basin and washed his hands of the whole affair. That's a cynic's way of conceding the debate.

Don't Retaliate When Insulted

Jesus, no doubt, had the mental capacity to heave back scorching insults to the cynics who scorned him on the day of his trial and crucifixion. If you don't believe it, ask the Pharisees and scribes who had been on the receiving end of his biting truth.

There are times when the cynics' shallowness needs to be exposed, not for the sake of cynics unlikely to be converted but for the sake of those being drained by them. But as Jesus came to his climactic moment, retaliation was inappropriate and even counterproductive. Heaping insult contributed nothing to Jesus' mission as Savior of the world.

When the cynics blister you, the temptation to retaliate bristles. You may be like Winston Churchill, in a famous encounter with Lady Astor. "Winston," she said, "if you were my husband, I would flavor your coffee with poison."

"Madam," the British leader replied, "if I were your husband, I would drink it."

You might have a burning desire to top the scorn of the cynic, but the result is simply an escalating, energy-consuming battle of wits.

Don't Threaten to Get Even

"While suffering, He uttered no threats," wrote Peter (1 Peter 2:23), who was there as Jesus headed for the cross.

The leader who threatens to even the score with cynics has cracked his own credibility and marred his own character.

"Walk worthy of [your] vocation," said Paul (Eph. 4:1 KJV). He spoke both of the general call of a person seeking to be Christlike and of the specific vocational call on a follower of Jesus Christ.

Getting even isn't true to the character of a Christ follower.

Trust Your Case to God

As leader of the Allied forces in World War II, General Dwight D. Eisenhower faced not only the Nazis but stern cynics in his own alliance. The British High Command felt "Ike" was in way over his head. Even Eisenhower's great friend General Omar Bradley "doubted his ability to properly manage a battlefield in combat."[7] When it was all said and done, however, "no one, not even his critics, questioned Eisenhower's most momentous achievement in the war" in forging and holding together a difficult alliance and leading it to victory over Nazi Germany.[8] Eisenhower understood a powerful principle that kept him from being drained: the cynics are not the final judges.

Jesus listened to the bitter taunts of the cynics as he faced a battle greater than World War II. But he entrusted himself to the judgment of his Father, not the opinions of cynics.

When the cynics' griefs and scorn scorch and blister, you must turn away, recognize you are seeking only the best, and trust yourself to God. His opinion is the only one that matters!

Keep Going Forward with Your Mission

Jesus, wrote Peter in the context of describing the cynical attitudes about him, "bore our sins in His body on the cross" (1 Peter 2:24). Jesus pressed on with his mission, undeterred by the cynics.

The real motive of the cynics—whether they acknowledge it or not—is to divert you from your mission. Jealousy, ideological disagreement, and strategic differences may compel them to try to burn up your path to victory.

The bottom line is this: heed the critics, consider the skeptics, but plow on in the face of the cynics.

7

DECEIVERS

Deceivers zap your energy by misleading you, so you spend precious time and resources going up a winding road to a dead end. Sometimes deceivers are not intentional in their shams and actually con themselves about their own motives.

Les, for example, wanted to learn more about his ministry area from Peace Mountain Church, a famed megachurch. He became friends with Dwayne, one of the church's pastors, while negotiating an internship at Peace Mountain.

One day Dwayne sensed he needed to have a frank conversation with Les. "Les, you're married with a young daughter," he noted. "Doing an internship with a family is hard." Dwayne arranged for Les to meet with another intern who had a family, and the intern explained the difficulties of raising support and caring for a family in a very expensive region.

Les decided the internship wasn't for him. In a phone call to Dwayne, he explained, "It'll be too hard to sell our house and raise support. We've prayed and don't sense God's leadership to undertake the internship."

"We all feel you would be a great asset to our team," Dwayne replied, "but I'm not going to try to talk you into coming."

Three weeks later, Les called again. "We've changed our minds," he said. "After praying some more, I feel coming to Peace Mountain for an internship is what God wants me to do."

The internships covered two years. Les resigned from the church he was serving, sold his home, and moved to Peace Mountain with his family.

Two months later, Les went to see Dwayne to tell him he had been offered a job in another department in the church. "Les, I love having you on the team, and I want what's best for you," Dwayne said. "If we can't have you in our area, at least you'll still be part of our church."

Later, in a chat with the administrator of the department where Les went to work, Dwayne got a shock. "We didn't ask Les to come work for us," he said. "After all, he was committed to intern with you. *Les* approached *us*."

Dwayne concluded Les had used him to get his foot in the door at Peace Mountain. After six months, Les showed up at Dwayne's office again. "I'm leaving Peace Mountain," he said. "I'm taking a job in the business world. For the last four years, I've been struggling about whether I wanted to be in full-time ministry. I don't know if I want to be a pastor anymore."

Les hadn't set out to deceive anyone. In his struggle for self-understanding, he had layered on one deception after another. The cynics delight in making you stew, but deceivers like Les intend no pain for you—yet that is often the result.

Two Types of Deceivers

One deceiver type practices *misinformation*, giving out information that is wrong but not because of a desire to mislead anyone.

Deceivers who purvey misinformation do so for several reasons. Like Les, some are confused about themselves and their situation. Other deceivers who deal out misinformation have misunderstood the source and simply pass along the bad information.

There are also the deceivers who confuse fact with fiction and create scenarios that have no relation to fact. The Internet has become such a hotline for misinformation that websites have been developed to separate fact from fiction.

The second category of deceiver transmits *disinformation* to mislead others purposely. The misinformer, then, may not have a malicious intent to deceive, while the disinformer almost always spreads false information knowingly.

Disinformation works in several ways. Sometimes the deceiver will put a *subtle spin* on actual facts that leads to wrong conclusions. The target—be it an individual, a group, a corporation, or a nation—has a distorted view of the situation, resulting in counterproductive and costly actions.

Another disinformation technique aims to manipulate people by causing them to *doubt* what they have believed or been told is true. One twist on this strategy is to build support for spurious ideas and scenarios.

A third disinformation ploy is the *cover-up*, in which crucial information is concealed. In free societies where media can't be censored, deceivers try to fill the communication channels with disinformation.

Disinformation kept the Cold War going and is among the factors breeding distrust in the Middle East. It drains individuals of hard-earned resources.

I (Wallace) was targeted by a deceiving scammer who said I owed "back taxes" to the "Department of Education."

I laughed at the scammer. "I am a former assistant director of the White House Cabinet Committee on Education, and I know the Department of Education does not 'tax' people directly. Its money comes from my income taxes, which are paid in full!"

In *The Da Vinci Code*, author Dan Brown uses fiction to suggest fallacies such as Jesus was married to Mary Magdalene. Whether a work of misinformation, in which Brown builds a fictional case based on his own incorrect reading of history, or of disinformation, through which the author tries to discredit Christianity, *The Da Vinci Code* is a striking example of how both styles of deception work.

Breeding Grounds for Deception

Organizational relationships are breeding grounds for both varieties of deception.

"Absence of trust" leads the list of "five dysfunctions of a team," according to management consultant Patrick Lencioni. Trust, he writes, "is the confidence among team members that their peers' intentions are good, and that there is no reason to be protective or careful around the group. In essence, teammates must get comfortable being vulnerable with one another."[1]

Lencioni describes the drain of the deceivers:

Teams that lack trust waste inordinate amounts of time and energy managing their behaviors and interactions within the group. They tend to dread team meetings, and are reluctant to take risks in asking for or offering assistance to others. As a result, morale on distrusting teams is usually quite low, and unwanted turnover is high.[2]

CEO offices of all types—from those of president of the United States to pastors of churches to heads of corporations—are always in danger of becoming chambers of deception.

Tragedy occurs when the front office becomes a chamber of deceit. Often it's not intentional. When the leader's quarters are cut off from the rest of the world, it tends to be populated with people who see things the same way and allow no opportunity for opposing truth to come through the mahogany doors.

As a young White House aide, I (Wallace) watched a deceptive atmosphere drain a president and bring down his administration. I sought to describe the atmosphere of the Nixon White House in a book I wrote in 1976, *The White House Mystique*.[3]

I described "the White House warp," in which "reality filters into the White House as through a prism . . . (and is) colored, distorted, bent as it flows from the day-by-day universe into a cosmos where the vulnerable feels invulnerable and the mediocre superior."[4]

Because I was a junior aide to the president, I didn't draw big assignments. I would be sent to small towns where people shopped in discount stores and considered an outing at a fast-food restaurant a special evening. But there I ran into truth at a level from which, it appeared to me, the Oval Office and its extended court had been cut off.

"You guys really need to get out of here and go meet the people," I remember telling some of my colleagues one day. My concern was they had begun to believe their own spin.

Jesus and the Deceivers

Jesus dealt with both misinformers and disinformers. The deceivers sought constantly to drain and discredit him. They failed because Jesus "knew what was in man" (John 2:25). He could see right through them and their deceptions.

Jesus and the Misinformers

Among the misinformed were the followers of John the Baptist. They had no desire to damage Jesus' reputation and ministry; they simply misunderstood. Some got into a theological discussion with a Jew regarding rites of purification. Apparently during the conversation there was mention of Jesus baptizing people.

> John's disciples came to him and said, "Teacher, the man you met on the other side of the Jordan River, the one you said was the Messiah, is also baptizing people. And everybody is going over there instead of coming here to us."
>
> John 3:26 NLT

John's friends were misinformed on two counts. First, Jesus himself was baptizing no one, but his disciples were (see John 4:2). Second, John's followers were misinformed about the distinction between John and Jesus. John had no such misperception and told them, "He must increase, but I must decrease" (John 3:30).

This shred of misinformation became a major issue by the time it reached the Pharisees. They saw that Jesus was baptizing more than John and used it as evidence that the Jesus movement was picking up speed. God's timing for the cross was precise. Jesus knew he must not emerge prematurely and give the Pharisees the opportunity to move against him precipitously. The misinformation caused Jesus to change his plans, leave Jerusalem, and travel to Galilee (see John 4:1–3).

Yet Jesus' interaction with John's disciples later shows us how to handle innocent misinformers. When John was in Herod's prison facing execution, he needed to ease his own mind that Jesus really was the Messiah. Some of his friends confronted Jesus: "Are You the Expected One, or do we look for someone else?" (Luke 7:20).

Jesus could have sighed in exasperation. Rather, he gave them the simple facts: "Go and report to John what you have seen and heard: the blind receive sight, the lame walk, the lepers are cleansed, and the deaf hear, the dead are raised up, the poor have the gospel preached to them" (Luke 7:22).

Jesus and the Disinformers

One evening after a long day's work, Jesus and his disciples sailed to the eastern side of the Sea of Galilee. When they arrived, Jesus' followers realized they forgot to bring bread for supper.

"Watch out and beware of the leaven of the Pharisees and Sadducees," he said (Matt. 16:6), as he listened to them worrying over the missing bread. They were confused, still focused on literal bread. Finally they understood Jesus was talking to them about "the teaching of the Pharisees and Sadducees" (v. 12).

Jesus teaches us that disinformation is to truth what leaven is to bread. To produce leaven, a baker takes a pinch of dough from a fresh batch and sets it aside, allowing it to ferment. Then the baker puts the fermented chunk in the next fresh lump of dough, and the leaven begins to infuse the mass with its nature.

Similarly, disinformation is often a smattering of truth separated out, spun, and twisted, then reinserted into public discourse. There it infuses its own nature—distortion and misunderstanding for the sake of harm.

It's Time for a Refill

When the deception seems as real as the truth.

Disinformation is a favorite tactic in warfare. It was crucial to the Allies' plan to invade Europe in 1944. A fake military camp was set up in a region of England that would cause the Germans to conclude the attack would be made farther up the coast from Normandy. The base included tanks and other heavy artillery, as well as trucks and Jeeps.

General George Patton—to his chagrin—was even appointed commander of a nonexistent army. Disinformation specialists generated radio traffic the Germans could intercept to give the appearance that units of Patton's force were talking to one another. The deception was carried off so skillfully that the German war leaders bought into it and focused their defenses around targets in the Pas-de-Calais zone, rather than at Normandy.

Deceivers—especially the disinformers—are always trying to get you to embrace their distortions as truth. Staying alert to their subtle misdirections, rumors, and misapplication of the facts is wearying. You're almost drained dry when their false armies and fake strategies seem to be genuine.

When the deception seems so powerful you lose sight of the truth.

This is the next level in the draining spiral of the deceivers. First, a leader mistakes fraud for fact, then loses sight of the truth altogether. When that occurs, leaders are near the bottom of the tank of their mental and emotional energies. This deception causes people and their organizations to disconnect from their original values, mission, and goals. Peter Drucker, in his epic study *Management*, says,

> Only a clear definition of the mission and purpose of the business makes possible clear and realistic business objectives. It is the foundation for priorities, strategies, plans, and work assignments. It is the starting point for the design of managerial jobs, and, above all, for the design of managerial structures. Structure follows strategy. Strategy determines what the key activities are in a given business.

And strategy requires knowing "what our business is and what it should be."[5]

When the deceivers surround you, your mission shifts to mere survival, and you're in danger of losing sight of why you and your team exist in the first place. When that happens, you lose not only your mission but all the elements that arise from it.

Dealing with Deceivers

Keep Your Eyes on the Light

Many years ago, I (Wallace) sailed with my wife and thirteen-month-old daughter on a freighter from America to Europe.

The wintry Atlantic was a sea of deception. The gray ocean merged with the gray sky, making it impossible to tell them apart. Fog often shrouded the vessel until the bow seemed to disappear. There were no landmarks, and the navigational stars were cloaked in the gloom. Yet the morning came when I arose and looked out my porthole window to see the lights of Rotterdam.

It turns out the captain and his helmsmen had a secret. One night I discovered it. Restless, I had left our small cabin and climbed to a position just above the ship's bridge. There I could see a pedestal crowned by a glass globe and bathed in a soft green light. Suddenly I realized I was looking at the ship's compass. (This was before satellite-based positioning systems.) The green light made the compass visible in the darkest night. No matter how thick the fog or how confusing the horizon, night or day, the captain and his crew kept their eyes on the light and kept us on course.

The deceivers cannot mislead you and your group if you keep your eyes on your values, vision, mission, and goals. Consider what each of these means:

1. Values—the people and principles for which you will sacrifice because you cherish them so highly
2. Vision—the way you want your world to look as it is aligned with your values
3. Mission—the overarching statement of what you will do to realize your vision
4. Goals—the specific things you will accomplish to achieve your mission

Jesus valued doing the will of his Father above all else. This brought on a cluster of other values: a love for people imprisoned by evil, a passion for righteousness, a desire to see truth win.

Jesus' vision was always focused on what the world would be like without sin. He knew Isaiah's description of a cosmos in which lion and lamb would lie together and in which swords were beaten into plows. He also could see in his divine heart the shape of the world to come if he continued on his redemptive mission.

Jesus' mission was to reconcile the world to the Father.

Jesus' goals were to glorify the Father, seek and save the lost, give his life as a ransom for many, and destroy the works of the evil one. The strategy was the cross. It was the only route to the open tomb and the world's redemption. Jesus had to keep his eyes on the light; otherwise the deceivers would shroud the truth until it disappeared.

Simon Peter, because of his own self-misinformed outlook, wanted Jesus to avoid the cross. As Jesus reveals to his followers the necessity of going to Jerusalem and dying, Peter takes him aside. "This will never happen to you!" Peter says (Matt. 16:22 NLT). The misinformed often are the prime spreaders of misinformation.

When the Pharisees tried to sidetrack Jesus through their disinformation, he continued his focus on his values, vision, mission, and goals.

Keep the Light on the Deceivers

Regarding the misinformer, illuminate the facts. When everyone else panics over rumors and the misinformation that feeds them, the leader has to keep the light on the facts.

Shifting markets rumble with misinformation, and many an organization has sunk in the tumult. Kmart found out the hard way that businesses cannot be operated on intuition, instinct, or assumptions about market needs and desires; they must be operated on facts. Investment watchers were stunned as the big retailer's stock plunged 25 percent in a two-day period, and plans were announced to close hundreds of stores. Self-nurtured misinformation was at the heart of the collapse, according to one analyst, as Kmart "came to believe in its own infallibility and lost track of where it really stood in the marketplace."[6]

The problem with the misinformer is he "thinks" he knows what the facts are. Often he's like the pilot who suffers vertigo, "thinks" he's right side up when he's upside down, and crashes. Kmart's management "believed that they had invented discount retailing and they knew best what the marketplace wanted."[7] But, as the company's collapse showed, that idea was an illusion based on misinformation about changes in the marketplace. The misinformed were in charge and spread their misinformation throughout the huge chain of stores.

Several times Jesus would have plowed into the ground had he let the misinformers drive his agenda. They had only a small fragment of the grand plan of God for the redemption of the cosmos. To have acted on the limited information would have sent the plan into a tailspin. Jesus had to keep the light on the facts of his vision and mission. The result was that the well-intentioned misinformers didn't wreck Jesus or their own destinies!

Regarding the disinformer, illuminate the fraud. Alicia was a bright young woman in my (Shaun) youth ministry who flirted with fraud.

Alicia had gone to the winter formal dance. "What did you do after the dance?" I asked her.

"We went back to my girlfriend's house and watched movies. But we were so tired we couldn't stay awake," she replied.

A few days later, Alicia's mother called. "Alicia lied to me," she said. "After the winter formal, she got drunk and had sex with a guy." I was crushed. Alicia had devised a disinformation scheme to perpetrate a fraud.

Casual incidents can become habits that set in as life-styles, so to save Alicia, the fraud had to be illuminated.

"Alicia, you lied to me about what happened after the winter formal," I said when she came to my office. Dismay crossed her face. "You must understand trust has to be earned," I continued. "It can take years to build trust but only one bad decision to destroy it."

The good news is that Alicia got the point. But the only way to help her was through the painful exposure of her fraud.

Jesus took no pleasure in illuminating the fraud going on in the temple. He loved the money changers whose tables he overturned, even as he was driving them out of the temple. In fact, they were people for whom he was willing to give his life. But the fraud had to be illuminated so people could see it in all its ugliness and danger.

Perhaps the illumination of fraud was also Jesus' intention when the religious disinformers brought him the woman caught in adultery. The Bible says he stooped down and wrote something in the dust. Some scholars believe it might have been the names of some of the woman's accusers who had had sexual relations with her!

Exposure of fraud is essential not only for helping those who carry it out but for the people affected by it.

Propaganda is a favorite device of the disinformers. American prisoners in North Vietnam's POW camps were forced to listen to communist propaganda spewing from loudspeakers for hours. Disinformation created tales designed to sap the POWs of their hope and soften them to accept the fraud spun by Marx.

Senator John McCain, for example, says that throughout every day in his North Vietnamese cell block, loudspeakers hanging from the ceiling blared songs from a propaganda specialist the prisoners called "Hanoi Hannah."[8] Similar propaganda had been spewed at Americans captured by the Chinese during the Korean War. A few of those prisoners actually bought into the fraud and defected.

Everyone today resides under the propaganda machines of a fallen culture. The lies flow seductively on morning television shows, movies, radio talk, the Internet, music, and pulpits that have lost the vision for biblical authority and truth.

The secret of the POWs who overcame the drain of the disinformers was twofold:

You must have truth to *recognize* the propaganda of the disinformers.

You must have truth to *refute* the propaganda of the disinformers—for yourself, if for no one else.

Jesus gives us the bottom line regarding the deceivers: "You will know the truth, and the truth will make you free" (John 8:32).

8

DEPRESSORS

Dale Carnegie sketched the profile of all depressor-drainers when he described Mary Todd Lincoln:

> Though at Madame Victorie Charlotte Le Clere Mentelle's school . . . she had been taught to dance the cotillion, she had been taught nothing about the fine art of handling people. So she took the surest way, the quickest way to annihilate a man's love: she nagged. She made Lincoln so uncomfortable that he wanted to avoid her.[1]

The nagging most often centered on what Mrs. Lincoln viewed as her husband's inadequacies. She found Lincoln crude in his dress and lifestyle, and she told him so. But, wrote Carnegie, "she didn't use any tact or diplomacy or sweetness in her telling."[2]

As Lincoln came to know Mary Todd more during their engagement, the reality of his circumstances began to sink in. And that plunged Lincoln into a deep depression. "Although he had definitely agreed to the marriage, his whole soul rebelled against it," wrote Carnegie. Lincoln's mind was in a "deep abyss."[3]

"Danny Depressor" Meets "Olivia Optimist"

Not long ago I (Shaun) thought the ghost of Mary Todd was hovering over a debriefing session following a discipleship retreat.

"The buses were late," said "Danny Depressor."

"But we got it all worked out, and we learned from the experience so we can be on top of it next year," replied "Olivia Optimist."

"The students had to wait so long they probably won't go next year," moaned Danny.

"But we had a record attendance," answered Olivia.

"Yeah, but we had more kids leave early because of the winter formal dance," Danny retorted.

Like Danny, some depressors believe they are helping by being problem solvers. There is indeed a place for constructive critiques. However, when the assessment comes through a depressor, you may feel you want to join old Abe in his "deep abyss."

But no matter how important it is to hear negative facts, it's even more important *not* to hear them negatively!

A critique from an upbeat, confident person will include promise and possibility. For the depressor, the mistake this year is terminal. Depressors are existentialists to the core, convinced the current moment and its mess-up are the sum total of all reality.

Dr. Judith Briles calls such people "energy suckers of life."[4] Her studies show that "working in a negative environment, surrounding yourself by negative people . . . can make you sick. Even deathly ill."[5]

By the way, unbridled optimism is not the answer to the depressors. Blind buoyancy can—forgive the oxymoron—

sink you too. Olivia Optimist will lead you merrily over the edge of a cliff. For her, there are no problems to be solved, no cliff out there, just a shiny, golden path to glory.

The draining depressor is a defeatist, but the blind optimist is deluded.

Jesus and the Depressors

To the shopkeepers, busy mothers, feisty school boys, and grim religious leaders in Nazareth, there was nothing extraordinary about Jesus, Joseph and Mary's kid. For three decades, the Nazareth townspeople had seen the stages of Jesus' growing-up years—a toddler at Mary's side at the well, a small lad playing in the sawdust in Joseph's carpentry shop, an adolescent serving as Joseph's errand boy, and a young adult working as Joseph's right-hand man.

Then one day at the Nazareth synagogue, he was chosen to be Sabbath reader. He picked up the Isaiah scroll and read the words,

> The spirit of the Lord is upon me, because he anointed me to preach the gospel to the poor. He has sent me to proclaim release to the captives, and recovery of sight to the blind, to set free those who are oppressed, to proclaim the favorable year of the Lord.
>
> Luke 4:18–19

Jesus closed the scroll, gave it back to the synagogue official, turned to the congregation, and said, in short, "That's *me*."

We can only imagine what the reaction might have been. Perhaps as people listened to Jesus speak, they had been thinking, *What a fine voice. How nice of a carpenter's helper to be able to read the synagogue lesson. How proud Mary must be.*

But Jesus didn't let it rest with that. "I'm the One this is all about," he said, in essence. More precisely, Jesus told his local crowd,

> Probably you will quote me that proverb, "Physician, heal yourself"—meaning, "Why don't you do miracles here in your hometown like those you did in Capernaum?" But the truth is, no prophet is accepted in his own hometown.
>
> Certainly there were many widows in Israel who needed help in Elijah's time, when there was no rain for three and a half years and hunger stalked the land. Yet Elijah was not sent to any of them. He was sent instead to a widow of Zarephath—a foreigner in the land.
>
> Luke 4:23–26 NLT

Call it "the Nazareth syndrome." Sadly, the Bible says of Nazareth that Jesus "did not many mighty works there because of their unbelief" (Matt. 13:58 KJV).

The Nazareth syndrome has two prongs. First, unbelief quenches the works of God. Second, the people who take you for granted usually don't see the possibilities in you and can become the biggest depressors in your life.

Sometimes the depressors will stop at nothing to hinder you. The Nazareth populace was so offended by Jesus, they tried to throw him off a cliff! The depressors in your life may not go to such extremes, but they will always try to plunge you to the bottom.

It's Time for a Refill

When the cloak of despair muffles your trumpet.

Your trumpet is the passion, mission, and goal that makes you get out of bed, put on your clothes, and charge into the day.

Depressors are shrouded in huge blankets usually wet with whining tears. Their cloaks are big enough for two, and they really want you under there with them. If you let them, they'll wrap you up in their dismal shroud until the trumpets are muffled. You begin to lose the motivation to pursue your vision.

As a young man, Solomon built empire, wealth, and a grand temple. But somewhere along the way, his examination of life led him to some pretty depressing conclusions.

> I, the Preacher, have been king over Israel in Jerusalem. And I set my mind to seek and explore by wisdom concerning all that has been done under heaven. It is a grievous task which God has given to the sons of men to be afflicted with. I have seen all the works which have been done under the sun, and behold, all is vanity and striving after wind. What is crooked cannot be straightened and what is lacking cannot be counted. I said to myself, "Behold, I have magnified and increased wisdom more than all who were over Jerusalem before me; and my mind has observed a wealth of wisdom and knowledge." And I set my mind to know wisdom and to know madness and folly; I realized that this also is striving after wind. Because in much wisdom there is much grief, and increasing knowledge results in increasing pain.
>
> Ecclesiastes 1:12–18

The trumpets summon us to God's journey for our lives.

I (Shaun) learned the value of the journey when I was a child. Our family would make visits to a favorite aunt and uncle four hours away. Almost always, I would fall asleep shortly into the drive. When we arrived at our destination, Dad, Mom, or my sister would be gabbing excitedly about interesting things they had seen on the way.

"Shaun, you missed the coolest thing," I can remember my father saying one time. He described the wonder that had passed before their eyes, and I wished I hadn't snoozed.

I was more focused on the destination than the journey. After the first few miles I was happy to doze off because it made the trek go faster. But when my family described the fascinating things along the road, I realized the wonders were revealed in the process of getting to the destination.

The journey is where we learn life's lessons and behold its delights. Miss the journey and you miss the joy of the pilgrimage.

When we allow the depressors to squelch our trumpets, we miss the journey. The only call we hear at the destination is taps, blown by a bugler. Trumpets are for the trip, bugles for the termination point.

Don't allow the depressing drainers to cause you to miss the journey by muffling your trumpets!

When your fuse fizzles.

In 1998, I (Wallace) despaired about America. I had left the political arena in 1973 and become a pastor. For a quarter century I not only served churches but studied the roots of nations. I received a fresh vision of the kingdom of God and of the distance that America had veered from the aims of her founders. I decided to resign as a pastor and run for Congress.

My campaign relied heavily on volunteers. I knew I had to protect them from the depressors who were barraging us in the media and from gossip campaigns at cocktail parties. Above all, I had to protect myself from the tides of despair with which we were doused daily by the depressors. If I allowed my fuse to go out, those who worked so hard for my election would be discouraged.

But there were days I had to fan furiously on the fuse to keep the spark lit. The Houston district where I was running for Congress was huge, and campaigning was costly. In the first months, I was in the top three of seven candidates in the polls, but then some of my competitors began to out-distance me in fund-raising. My fuse burned low when I realized the $190,000 we would spend on the campaign was paltry beside the budgets of some of my opponents. Yet I couldn't let down the people who had sacrificed to help me make the run. Daily I had to resist the depressors who suggested we didn't have a chance.

When the voting was finished, I didn't win, yet I *did* win. My mission was to be an ambassador of the kingdom with its transforming message in the crumbling political arena, and I had been able to do that. The man who won appointed me his acting chief of staff, and I spent the next year helping him set up his offices in Houston and Washington. Then I returned to my central call—the church.

When you can barely see out of the rut you're in.

In the Bible, Job initially resisted the depressing drainers. When word came that a tornadic wind brought the house down on his kids, Job's response was, "Naked I came from my mother's womb, and naked I shall return there. The LORD gave and the LORD has taken away. Blessed be the name of the LORD" (Job 1:21). The Bible is careful to note, "Through all this Job did not sin nor did he blame God" (Job 1:22).

Later, however, after wearying weeks of advice from the depressing drainers, Job sunk low. His rut became so deep he could barely see out of it, and he cried,

> Let the day perish on which I was to be born,
> And the night which said, "A boy is conceived."
> May that day be darkness;
> Let not God above care for it,
> Nor light shine on it.
> Let darkness and black gloom claim it;
> Let a cloud settle on it;
> Let the blackness of the day terrify it.

As for that night, let darkness seize it;
  Let it not rejoice among the days of the year;
  Let it not come into the number of the months.
Behold, let that night be barren;
  Let no joyful shout enter it.
Let those curse it who curse the day,
  Who are prepared to rouse Leviathan.
Let the stars of its twilight be darkened;
  Let it wait for light but have none,
  And let it not see the breaking dawn;
Because it did not shut the opening of my mother's
  womb,
  Or hide trouble from my eyes.

Job 3:3–10

When your rut is that low, you are in danger of sinking to its bottom, and it becomes difficult to crawl out.

Dealing with Depressors

Give the Depressors a History Lesson

When Jesus declared his mission at the Nazareth synagogue (see Luke 4), there were many messianic prophecies he could have read. But he wanted the people to understand clearly what he had come to do. Jesus chose Isaiah because the moment was definitive.

Each Old Testament prophet had a role in profiling the coming Messiah, and Isaiah's was to detail his nature. He wouldn't be a galloping knight or a gallant prince or a graven sage, but rather a suffering servant, a man of sorrows, one acquainted with grief who would be despised and rejected of men (see Isaiah 53).

So not only was Jesus announcing his own mission, he was also reconnecting the people at the synagogue with their own historic tradition about the Messiah.

A favorite refrain of the depressors is "You're not up to the job. It's too big for you. You're overestimating your own strengths and talents!" Jesus' point to the Nazareth citizenry was the historic truth that the Messiah would seem insignificant but would accomplish much.

Over the next three years, Jesus would make crude fishermen into eloquent spokesmen for the kingdom of God, transform cold politicians into sensitive and compassionate servants, and turn skeptics into martyrs. Across history, the boy from the carpenter's shop would ignite an inside-out, bottom-up revolution of the human spirit that would topple empires.

When the depressors say it can't be done or you're too small for the shoes you're trying to wear, remind them of history. Reacquaint them with William Wilberforce, who cried out in the British Parliament for two decades for the end of the slave trade until it happened. Recall for the depressing drainers the struggles of Hudson Taylor in China and how the booming church there is a modern testimony to his unseen labors. Don't let the depressors lose memory of David Livingstone hacking his way through African jungles, or of a miniscule Albanian nun the world knew as Mother Teresa.

Nail Down the Generalizers

Draining depressors are generalizers. *All* salesmen are sleazy, *all* lawyers are shysters, *all* politicians are pork-barrelers, and *all* preachers are egomaniacs.

Peter Murphy, a peak performance expert, says, "If my friend says all dogs are aggressive I will ask him: Small dogs or big dogs? All dogs or certain breeds? . . . In what kind of situations? By doing this you can shift the perspective of the negative person from a generalized overreaction to a highly specific opinion. This will ease some of the negativity and the intensity of their outburst."[6]

"Physician, heal yourself" was a generalized challenge negative folk would sometimes throw at a person who fit their perceptions of a charlatan. Jesus knew what was in their minds, so he got specific. He reminded them of how wrong the Israelites had been about Elijah. They had figured that if one prophet lied, they must all be liars, and that attitude had sent him to aid "foreigners," the people who would receive him.

Depressors assume that if you have one flaw, your whole personality is messed up. Nail down the depressing drainers by helping them focus on specifics.

Ask for Their Authority

When generalizers say that "all dogs are aggressive," Murphy says to ask them, "According to who?"[7]

Authority was a big issue for the depressing drainers around Jesus. They tried constantly to muddle Jesus by asking him to tell them the authority by which he forgave sins, healed the sick, and sent demons scurrying for cover. They showed their own misunderstanding of authority when they accused Jesus of casting out demons by the power of the prince of demons, Satan (see Matt. 12:24). But Jesus turned the tables on the depressing drainers.

> "I'll tell you who gave me the authority to do these things if you answer one question," Jesus replied. "Did John's baptism come from heaven or was it merely human?"
>
> They talked it over among themselves. "If we say it was from heaven, he will ask why we didn't believe him. But if we say it was merely human, we'll be mobbed, because the people think he was a prophet." So they finally replied, "We don't know."
>
> And Jesus responded, "Then I won't answer your question either."
>
> Matthew 21:24–27 NLT

Jesus knew the drainers could cite no authority for their opinions about John the Baptist. He was confident in the authority he had from his Father but knew the generalizers couldn't produce an equally credible source for their conclusions. So when Jesus asked them a question for which they would have to give an authoritative foundation, they were silenced.

Any belief system stands or falls on its authority—or lack of it. When the depressing drainers come at you with their morbid reasoning, despairing counsel, and hopeless viewpoints, ask them, "According to who?"

If They Don't Get It, Walk Right through Them

How did Jesus handle the depressors? He walked right through them. "Jumping up, they mobbed him and took him to the edge of the hill on which the city was built. They intended to push him over the cliff, but he slipped away through the crowd and left them" (Luke 4:29–30 NLT).

As you deal with the depressing drainers in your life, first walk right through their negativity with a positive attitude. Refuse to allow their dour opinions to sap your enthusiasm. It's as if their wall of pessimism isn't there. Second, recognize there are some people who won't catch your vision and won't go forward with you. Many of those folks you must turn loose.

However, there may be some depressing drainers you shouldn't turn loose. Jesus didn't cut loose Simon Peter the denier, Thomas the doubter, or even Judas the cynic. He didn't sever the bond with his misunderstanding mother or break off friendship with task-driven Martha. Abraham Lincoln didn't divorce Mary Todd Lincoln. Despite trendy social philosophies, you don't divorce your kids—and they can be real drainers sometimes.

The depressing drainers you do *not* cut loose are those with whom you are in covenant. A covenant relationship is one held together by a solemn, sacred agreement. Marriage is a covenant. Family ties adhere by the covenant God established through his sovereignty. You likely didn't select who would be in your family except for your spouse. All families include drainers, but you don't cut them off, even though they sap you.

"Incompatibility" is a reason many couples give for divorce. When marriage is viewed merely as a contract, the lack of a good match is viewed as legitimate grounds for breaking up. But in a covenant marriage, "incompatibility" doesn't count.

If you have a spouse, a parent, a child, or someone else in your immediate family who is a depressing drainer, remember that God may have put you with that person to provide him or her "lift."

I (Wallace) grew up in a dysfunctional home and needed that lift. Early in life I learned how to be a depressing drainer. I married Irene when I was nineteen and she was eighteen. I knew God had given me a wonderful gift. And from the perspective of more than forty years, I can see just how valuable a treasure God gave me in her. She has been his instrument in providing me lift, helping me get free of the depressing drainer lifestyle. Thank God she didn't give up on me!

There will be depressing drainers in your covenant circle who won't respond to your efforts to provide lift. There are a couple of actions you can take.

First, steel yourself for every encounter. As a bright young man, Daniel braced himself as he was hauled off to Babylon as a captive. There the Chaldeans—the watchdogs of Babylonian culture—wanted to brainwash the promising teen with their worldview. But he set his mind in concrete that he would not be "defiled" by the depressing drainers (see Dan. 1:8). Steeling yourself means following Daniel's example and determining beforehand that you will not be emptied of your convictions and values and refilled with those of fallen society.

Second, determine you'll go forward with positive actions despite the dour predictions of the depressing drainers. Daniel didn't want to defile himself with the diet specified by Babylon's King Nebuchadnezzar. Instead, he and Hananiah, Mishael, and Azariah would eat only vegetables. Rather than drinking Nebuchadnezzar's rich wine, Daniel and his friends would drink only water.

This news shook the bureaucrat designated to carry out the king's orders. He was convinced that Daniel and his compatriots would get so haggard on such a diet that the king would think his assistant wasn't enforcing his order. But Daniel persisted, and "at the end of ten days their appearance seemed better and they were fatter than all the youths who had been eating the king's choice food" (Dan. 1:15).

Daniel's determination not to yield to the king's despairing assistant established the young man as a person of uncompromising character.

Like Daniel and the king's assistant, sometimes there will be depressors with whom you are not in covenant relationship. As a man or woman who takes Jesus Christ seriously, do all possible to build them up. And if you must pull the plug on the relationship before they pull the plug on your tank of vitality, do it in a Christlike manner.

"Let all things be done for edification," wrote Paul (1 Cor. 14:26). And that includes the way you separate from the depressing drainers. Tell them lovingly why you are breaking the relationship and how they can be healed.

Don't be a depressing drainer yourself. Leave them with hope!

9

DISAPPOINTERS

One night I (Shaun) went with my wife, Teresa, to a beach-side restaurant near our community. Strolling toward the eatery, we spotted kids loitering around a car. Their loud voices blazed the night with foul speech. Clouds of cigarette smoke cloaked their faces, but we could see the youngsters were gulping alcohol.

"That makes me so sad to see students hanging out in a parking lot on Friday night drinking," I said to Teresa.

My gaze bore in on the young people as I tried to pierce the tobacco haze and see their faces. A break in the smoke gave me a glimpse. Suddenly my sadness became greater.

I was staring into the face of Kelly Ann, a star player in our youth ministry. The glowing young woman never missed a service, was always the first to sign up for retreats, and was willing to do whatever was asked, from arranging chairs to running the copy machine. I had great hopes Kelly Ann would go a long way in serving Christ. I was sure she would wind up in full-time ministry.

As I gaped at her in disbelief, her eyes connected with mine. As soon as she recognized me, Kelly Ann dashed behind the car, trying to hide.

My appetite faded and was replaced by a sick feeling. I've been in youth ministry long enough that not many things shock me anymore, but the disappointment I felt over Kelly Ann was devastating.

After staying away a month or so, she returned to church, but she would walk past me without saying a word. One day I stopped her. "Kelly Ann, I want you to know nothing has changed in my and Teresa's love for you. We're ready to talk—and listen—anytime you desire."

Kelly Ann went off to college, and Teresa and I moved to another state. Though that Friday night happened years ago, I still feel the disappointment. I pray somehow Kelly Ann got back on track for Christ and that she's serving him, finding joy and fulfillment in putting her abundant gifts to work.

Profile of Disappointers

Rick Morrissey, writing for the *Chicago Tribune*, sketched the profile of disappointers in a column about Bode Miller, who represented the United States in ski competitions during the 2006 Winter Olympics.

Miller, a confessed partier, failed to win Olympic gold—or silver or bronze. Morrissey's column was headlined, "Fittingly, Bode exits in a blaze of nothing." Morrissey quoted Miller, who said at the end of the winter games, "It has been an awesome two weeks. . . . I got to party and socialize at an Olympic level."

"If he had an awesome Olympics, then France had an awesome World War II" was Morrissey's wry comment.[1]

Even a strong leader like Billy Graham had to deal with disappointment. Someday, when historians get the full profile of

Graham, they will understand the special call God gave him for ministering to leaders. Graham has been criticized because he gave himself to people from both ends of the spectrum and every niche within it. Whether it was Democrats Lyndon Johnson and Bill Clinton or Republicans Dwight Eisenhower and Richard Nixon, Graham was ready to serve.

I (Wallace) watched from a not-too-distant seat as Dr. Graham sought to help Richard Nixon. The evangelist put himself on the line for the president and wound up deeply disappointed.

During the Watergate scandal, tapes were discovered that had recorded almost everything spoken in the Oval Office, including Nixon's gutter language. Graham had never heard the president use such foul speech.

"On the day the contents of the White House tapes were made public, and I heard the president's words, I was deeply distressed," Graham would write years later. "I felt physically sick and went into the seclusion of my study at the back of the house. Inwardly, I felt torn apart."[2]

Why We Disappoint

Why do people disappoint us? The better question is, why do we tear each other apart with disappointment? Whenever I (Wallace) entered that sparkling "honeymoon" period in serving a new congregation, I would always tell the people up front, "I don't want to disappoint you, but probably at some point I will."

Call it "negative confession," but I know myself. And that's a major reason we disappoint one another. We all have flaws. Those close to us will be let down.

But another reason disappointment drains is because, as author Stephen Covey says, "Each of us comes into a situation with expectations."[3] Our anticipations constitute a "should" map, he says, rather than an "is" map.

Often we assume others understand what we expect. Covey writes, "Implicit expectations are the problem." They are the "baggage" we carry into every relationship and interaction. The answer, Covey says, is to make explicit what we expect from employees and others with whom we are linked.[4]

The "Pygmalion effect" is another reason we disappoint one another. In Greek myth, the sculptor Pygmalion carved the statue of a beautiful woman and fell in love with the stone image. Through the power of passion, he gave it life.

So we project our own perspective on people, and when they are not transformed into our desired image, we are disappointed. Disappointment is kissing the woman to bring her to life only to find she's still a statue. When we impose our expectations on others, we set ourselves up for disappointment.

Jesus and the Disappointers

In Gethsemane, Jesus is approaching the apex of his purpose for coming into the world. The baptism of fire is about to be poured out on him (see Luke 12:50). He wants—needs—his best buddies to walk alongside him as he comes to his climactic moment.

Matthew reports the disappointing scene:

Then Jesus came with them to a place called Gethsemane, and said to His disciples, "Sit here while I go over there and pray." And He took with Him Peter and the two sons of Zebedee, and began to be grieved and distressed. Then He said to them, "My soul is deeply grieved, to the point of death; remain here and keep watch with Me." . . .

And He came to the disciples and found them sleeping, and said to Peter, "So, you men could not keep watch with Me for one hour? Keep watching and praying that you may not enter into temptation; the spirit is willing, but the flesh is weak." . . .

Again He came and found them sleeping, for their eyes were heavy. And He left them again, and went away and prayed a third time, saying the same thing once more. Then He came to the disciples and said to them, "Are you still sleeping and resting? Behold, the hour is at hand and the Son of Man is being betrayed into the hands of sinners. Get up, let us be going; behold, the one who betrays Me is at hand!"

Matthew 26:36–38, 40–41, 43–46

Jesus is draped over the rock, weeping and bleeding; his pals are cradled on another stone, snoring.

To what can we compare the disappointment the Lord must have felt? Maybe a child whose parent sleeps through his or her wedding. Perhaps a man whose spouse dozes as his community names him Man of the Year.

No comparisons come close. Jesus is about to stare into hell itself. The sins of the billions of earth's inhabitants across all history are about to be laid on him—a weight only he can carry.

But he needs his friends. The Lord of the universe needs his pals' arms around his shoulders, their tears to mingle with his. All he gets is the slobbery snorts of sleep.

For three years, Jesus has been preparing his men for this moment. He has weathered the disappointment of those who had turned away. Now the ones who stuck with him, the friends he could count on, fall asleep.

It's Time for a Refill

When you're ready to give up on the human race.

When the faces of disappointers stack up before you like a mountain range and you conclude there is no one left who will not let you down, the disappointers have just about emptied your vitality tank.

You know you're almost drained when you become a generalizer. "Men are insensitive blockheads!" says a woman whose last drop of romance has been tapped by a two-timer. "Women are impossible!" runs the converse from an exasperated Romeo.

When you find yourself lumping all people in a big trash bag of generality, the disappointers have gotten to you.

When you feel yourself morphing into a cynic.

I (Shaun) love to speak. I enjoy talking to people personally, but I especially love talking to groups about following Jesus Christ.

Several years ago, I passed through a shaky period. I was never satisfied with my messages. I was the opposite of the preacher in the old joke who said to his wife, "You know, dear, there are only five great preachers in the world." She replied, "There's one less than you think there is." I was so unsure about myself I would have figured I was at the bottom five of all in history who had ever stood in a pulpit. During that season, I would go home in a terrible mood. I felt like no one was connecting with the teachings and sermons.

Teresa is my most dependable and helpful critic. She will always tell me the truth. At times during my era of self-doubt, Teresa said, "That was a great message and delivery," and I mumbled some grim retort.

One weekend a member of the congregation approached me and said, "That message you preached really touched my heart." And I was thinking, *No, it didn't. You had to have been listening to someone else.*

My own expectations and fear of disappointing God and my congregation had drained me. Each Sunday I felt I had to top the previous message. When it didn't measure up to my expectations, I was disappointed. In turn, the disappointment made me cynical about myself and the compliments of those trying to encourage me.

What finally stopped the drain of disappointment was the realization *my* expectations weren't the ones that mattered. God asked my best. I knew week by week I was giving study, prayer, and delivery of the message my best efforts. By that standard, God was never disappointed. That awareness refilled my vitality tank, and I was excited once more to be in the pulpit.

When you begin to doubt even your trusted sidekicks.

What would the Lone Ranger be without Tonto, Laurel without Hardy, Quixote without Panza, Sheriff Andy without Deputy Fife, or Abbott without Costello?

Yet the disappointment you experience is siphoning your emotional energy when you want to put distance between you and even your most trusted companions.

In July 1946, a comic named Jerome Levitch teamed with an Italian crooner named Dino Crocetti at the 500 Club on Atlantic City's Boardwalk. For the next decade, they would zoom to stardom as Jerry Lewis and Dean Martin.

Lewis was a controller. Martin was a laid-back "whatever" person. Eventually Lewis's penchant for control drained Martin. On top of that, each of them was being filled with the notion that his partner was keeping him from greater things. The drain was too much, and Martin and Lewis split. For years they didn't speak to one another.[5]

There are probably people in your life you consider soul mates. When people see that person, they automatically think of you, and vice versa. It may be a spouse, a member of your church or group, a classmate, or a work partner. But when disappointment with your wider universe weighs down and threatens to divide that closest relationship, you're almost out of inner vitality.

Dealing with Disappointers

Call the Disappointers to Their Best

When Jesus finds his closest partners sleeping at his—and humanity's—crucial moment, he challenges them with a question: "Couldn't you watch with me just one hour?" (see Matt. 26:40).

In Greek, the word *watch* means to be fully awake and in a state of alertness. It is the peak of attentiveness. It is the best one can bring to being ready and on guard.

Jesus comes to the disappointers and reminds them of their best while summoning them to it.

Coach Randolph understood the principle. No player on his football team seemed to have more potential than Lance, yet none of the players disappointed him more often.

Coach Randolph was tenacious, never wanting to give up on a young player. Yet Lance—a running back—seemed not to be able to run without tripping over his own feet. It had become a joke to the rest of the team.

One day it occurred to Coach Randolph that Lance might do better in another position. He began to study the young man's build—his long arms and big, lean hands. The coach decided to assign Lance to play the receiving end position. Lance went on to become an award-winning receiver.

The disappointers in your midst might not be achieving their best because they've not been challenged to top performance or perhaps they're not playing the right position. Call them to their best, and give them an opportunity to shine.

Recognize the Deep Cause of Disappointing Behavior

Jesus is disappointed in his sleeping friends, but he doesn't fire them. He knows they are mere mortals whose bodies will wear out and whose eyes will sag in sleep. He doesn't give up on them, and they become history changers in his hands.

Jesus' handling of the snoozing disciples shows us it's vital to understand why people fail to meet our expectations.

I (Wallace) saw this truth demonstrated when I attended an exhibition of marching and dancing put on by my grand-daughter's high school. Hundreds of kids participated from throughout the school district. Among the dancers from one of the schools was a teen with Down syndrome. She was having a ball. She waved at family and friends, tried to stay in step, and was guided by her classmates.

Had her instructor expected perfection from the young woman, there would have been disappointment. But although she made mistakes, the young woman gave excellence to the presentation and to the evening.

Take Them as Far as They Will Go

A major question that night when the disciples fell asleep at history's catalytic moment was how far they would go with Jesus. If they had disappointed him in Gethsemane, would they let him down at Golgotha?

To answer that question, you must know the limits of individual disappointers. They wouldn't have disappointed you in the first place if they had not been people on whom you thought you could depend. But it's vital to be realistic about your team members, or you will be crushed.

While Jesus is disappointed his followers can't stay awake, he isn't in despair. He is realistic about their limitations. After they come to their rude, stark awakening by the clatter of armor and angry voices, they haul themselves out of the garden, leaving Jesus and only one other "disciple": Judas Iscariot.

Later John, in wrenching sorrow, makes it to the foot of the cross with Mary, Jesus' mother, on his arm. But the rest are hiding in the boonies. The key man, Simon Peter, is off somewhere in a heap of dust, turning it to mud with tears over his disappointment in himself.

As Jesus hangs on the cross, the sorrow of humanity's sin doesn't push aside his heartbreak over followers who couldn't be found, and he still hears the stinging words of his closest associate, spoken to a servant girl in Caiaphas's yard: "I do not know the man!" (Matt. 26:74).

The disciples aren't willing to come to Skull Hill. They don't show the same courage and faithfulness of Jesus' mother and Mary Magdalene, who were at the cross *and* the tomb. Jesus knows the disciples' limits and will not push them beyond the place they can walk. He forgives them, and they are the first people—after the women—he goes to see when he steps out of the grave.

It's important to be realistic about your expectations of the people you lead. Then, when they disappoint you, you won't give up on them. Rather, you'll go back to where they stopped and help them take baby steps forward until they are running toward their top performance and highest goals.

Go Forward without Them If You Must

Jesus turns toward his friends in Gethsemane, and the team has bolted. He turns again, this time toward his captors. His betrayal and arrest have "taken place to fulfill the Scriptures," he tells them (Mark 14:49). He has the option of halting the tragic scene. Jesus may not have any humans on his side as he faces the cross, but he can call on legions of angels.

Yet he does not. The disappointers have thudded up against the wall of their fears, but Jesus will keep going forward, straight to the cross.

Sadly, there will be disappointers who won't even respond to your help. You may have to leave some sitting back at the place of their failure. But you cannot let the disappointers hold you back.

Sir Alexander Mackenzie didn't. A decade before Lewis and Clark made their epic journey across America to the

Pacific, Mackenzie, a Canadian, trekked across his native land to the great western ocean.

Mackenzie had tried it once before in 1789, but that journey ran into a dead end of disappointment. The Mackenzie expedition had sought a water route to the Pacific. They discovered a powerful, broad river and struggled through it in their boats, fueled by their anticipation.

But the mighty river emptied into the Arctic Ocean, not the Pacific. Though the river would be named for him someday, in his diary Mackenzie scribbled the name he thought it ought to have: River of Disappointment.[6]

There may be seasons when you feel you're swimming in that waterway. Disappointment may be cresting around you, full of the whitecaps of failed expectations. And along the way, some of your mates may abandon ship. But the only way to make the voyage count is to get to the destination that matters—the fulfillment of your vision, purpose, mission, and goals.

Take as many with you as you can on the expedition toward success, but don't let the disappointers keep you from moving forward.

10

DISTRACTERS

I (Shaun) once worked with Clyde, a distracted distracter. He had little initiative and required micromanagement. To tell the truth, Clyde left me in a puddle of exhaustion after every encounter.

A parent called me, alarmed that her son, Larry, might be straying into bad company. I asked Clyde to take Larry to lunch. Kids believed in him and opened up in his presence. I felt Clyde was just the man to handle the need.

"I'd love to take Larry to lunch!" Clyde said.

Two days later my phone rang. It was Larry's dad. "My wife said someone from your staff would contact our son. The situation is getting bad, and we're desperate."

I apologized and headed straight for Clyde's desk. "I'm sorry," he said. "I'll get right on it."

A couple weeks later, right after a worship service, a woman approached me, weeping. "I'm Larry's mom," she said. "My son's in a lot of trouble. We've asked you for help, and you've promised, but nothing has happened!"

I realized I had made a mistake. I had trusted a distracted distracter to carry out this vital task. Clyde was like the chief ape on a zoo's monkey island. He was always leaping from branch to branch, taking many with him. He would forget assignments as his eyes glinted toward the next adventure. Unless I monitored his every step, his responsibilities wouldn't get done.

Not only did I have to try to get him back on task, but somehow I had to lasso all those who had followed him on his merry adventures and whose work had been left undone.

The Drain of Distraction

When leaders allow the distracters to drain them, the whole enterprise is in trouble. Colin Powell says, "When everyone's mind is dulled or distracted the leader must be doubly vigilant."[1]

I (Wallace) knew I had to be vigilant when I began my career in the newspaper business in the late 1960s. Computers were little more than science fiction fantasy. Back in those days, the city room of a newspaper was a clattering, clanging barrage of noise and demanded intense concentration. Accuracy could fly away on the winds of distraction. Get a fact wrong, and the newspaper could be sued and you could be pounding the pavement, looking for a new job.

Sometimes, to train reporters, a journalism teacher would assign students to write stories while the teacher read aloud from an exciting novel. The student had to learn to maintain the proper focus amidst the din.

The problem exists in organizations of all kinds. One report found that of the individuals surveyed, "Two-thirds are distracted 11 to 40 times a day, with a third receiving 21 or more interruptions."[2]

There isn't a stay-at-home mom alive who doesn't know the drain of distraction. Crying babies, simmering pots and pans, soccer schedules, parent-teacher meetings, needy spouses, dirty floors, civic responsibilities, and social occasions all prod, pull, and poke at her incessantly.

Jesus and the Distracters

The key problem of the distracters is they lose sight of the big picture in their fascination with the details. Such is the problem at the house of Simon the Pharisee:

> Now one of the Pharisees was requesting Him [Jesus] to dine with him, and He entered the Pharisee's house and reclined at the table. And there was a woman in the city who was a sinner; and when she learned that He was reclining at the table in the Pharisee's house, she brought an alabaster vial of perfume, and standing behind Him at His feet, weeping, she began to wet His feet with her tears, and kept wiping them with the hair of her head, and kissing His feet and anointing them with the perfume. Now when the Pharisee who had invited Him saw this, he said to himself, "If this man were a prophet He would know who and what sort of person this woman is who is touching Him, that she is a sinner." . . .
>
> Turning toward the woman, [Jesus] said to Simon, "Do you see this woman? I entered your house; you gave Me no water for My feet, but she has wet My feet with her tears and wiped them with her hair. You gave Me no kiss; but she, since the time I came in, has not ceased to kiss My feet. You did not anoint My head with oil, but she anointed My feet with perfume. For this reason I say to you, her sins, which are many, have been forgiven, for she loved much; but he who is forgiven little, loves little." Then He said to her, "Your sins have been forgiven."
>
> Luke 7:36–39, 44–48

The Pharisee's motive for having Jesus for dinner might be driven by curiosity or a desire to "check out" Jesus. Whatever the case, he doesn't extend common courtesies, such as providing foot-washing water, to his dinner guest.

And when the wretched woman darts into the dining room and begins washing and perfuming his feet, wiping them with her hair, the Pharisee mumbles. He is distracted from the need of the sinner by her presumptuous, impetuous act that brings embarrassment to his dinner party.

Jesus asks Simon, "Do you *see* this woman?" The distracter is yanked away from the person by political correctness and convention. Jesus then reminds Simon what he should have been focused upon. If he is insulted by the presence of a prostitute at his dinner table, he should also be embarrassed by his own failure to show proper courtesy to his guest. As you judge, you will be judged (see Matt. 7:2).

But the distracter does not pull Jesus' eyes away from the woman. "Your sins are forgiven," he tells her.

Sin is a major cause of distraction. In fact, there is something of the distracter in most of us. We would all prefer to skip the sin discussion. It is too close to home, for "all have sinned and fall short of the glory of God" (Rom. 3:23).

Poor Simon attempts to distract Jesus away from the woman and toward propriety. Perhaps he knows that the illuminating torch of Jesus' truth might bring to light his own sin.

Distraction happens again at Bethany.

Jesus, therefore, six days before the Passover, came to Bethany where Lazarus was, whom Jesus had raised from the dead. So they made Him a supper there, and Martha was serving; but Lazarus was one of those reclining at the table with Him. Mary then took a pound of very costly perfume of pure nard, and anointed the feet of Jesus and wiped His feet with her hair; and the house was filled with the fragrance of the perfume. But Judas Iscariot, one of His disciples, who was intending to betray Him, said, "Why was this perfume not sold for three hundred denarii and given to poor people?" Now he said this, not because he was concerned about the poor, but because he was a thief, and as he had the money box, he used to pilfer what was put into it. Therefore Jesus said, "Let her alone, so that she may keep it for the day of My burial. For you always have the poor with you, but you do not always have Me."

John 12:1–8

In the first episode, there is a distraction away from sin and the sinner and toward social convention. In the second, the distraction is turning attention away from the Savior and toward the cost of the perfume.

Judas is so distracted by the budget, he forgets the big picture.

We still run into those kinds of distracters. In the 1960s I (Wallace) was youth pastor of a church in Fort Worth, Texas. We had installed a skating rink in the cavernous basement below the sanctuary. On Friday nights the concrete floors and walls bounded with the gleeful noise of young people zipping around the course, munching refreshments, and listening to music.

Everybody was happy but Grady, the building superintendent.

The corridors surrounding the great worship center upstairs were inlaid with rich tile. Large squares in a checkerboard pattern dressed the hallways. Grady polished them relentlessly. The gleaming tile corridors were his badge of honor. But the hordes of galloping teenagers had to cross his gleaming tile to get to the stairs and elevator that would take them down to the basement skating area. Scuff marks were everywhere as Grady inspected the buildings on Saturday, preparing for Sunday.

One day in a staff meeting, Grady complained about what the Friday night youth gatherings were doing to his shining floors. He would have preferred we cancel the activity. Grady was more focused on the costly floors than the kids. The senior pastor, however, understood the impact of the activity on the teens' lives, and we were able to continue the ministry.

Jesus also refuses to follow distractions. At the house of Simon the Pharisee, Jesus does not turn away from the needy woman, though his host is offended. Nor does he let Simon off the hook, but he reminds him of his own offense.

And at Bethany, Jesus has eyes only for the cross and the mission of humanity's redemption. From that, he will not be distracted.

It's Time for a Refill

When you get preoccupied with the distractions.

Os Guinness, in his book *The Devil's Gauntlet*, recounts the story of a skillful distraction during the communist era in the old Soviet Union.

A guard in a Leningrad lumber mill knew the workers there were filching materials. One day Pyotr Petrovich emerged from his shift pushing a wheelbarrow carrying a hefty sack.

"What have you got there?" the guard barked.

"Just sawdust and shavings," Petrovich replied.

"I wasn't born yesterday," said the guard. "Tip it out."

Petrovich dumped the sack on the ground. Sawdust and wood shavings fell out.

For a full week, Petrovich left work pushing the wheelbarrow containing the sack. Finally the guard had enough. "I know you. Tell me what you're smuggling out of here, and I'll let you go!"

Petrovich smiled. "Wheelbarrows, my friend, wheelbarrows."[3]

When all you can see is a bag of dust, the distracters have almost depleted your mental focus.

When one light begins to look as good as another.

Many years ago, I (Wallace) found myself in a small private aircraft on July 4. The pilot and I were flying the short distance from Tyler, Texas, to Love Field in Dallas.

As we approached Dallas around 9:30 p.m., celebratory fireworks began to explode in front of and below us. One of the pilots, a World War II veteran, remarked on how it reminded him of bombing runs over German cities.

That did nothing to soothe my frayed nerves. I was already wondering how he would sort out the airport's lights from all the other glitter on the Dallas landscape stretching out for miles. The fireworks only added to the confusion. Down there somewhere was the light that would signal the approach to Love Field, and I—who knew little of piloting—could only pray we could find it and not be misled by all the other beams, beacons, and brilliances. Thankfully, the pilot knew how to tell the genuine light from all its competitors, and we landed safely.

The glittering distractions all tempt you to get your eyes off your guiding light. When all beacons seem to lead to your destination, the distracters threaten the last of your soul's vitality.

Masses of people today, for example, are drained of spiritual vitality by all the religions promising heaven. Jesus says, "I am the way, and the truth, and the life; no one comes to the Father but through me" (John 14:6).

This is the one Light from which we must not be distracted, no matter how titillating the others.

When sunrises are confused as sunsets.

When the authorities, led by Judas, arrested Jesus in the Garden of Gethsemane, his followers assumed the sun had set on their day of opportunity. Jesus was being hauled off to execution.

The distracters will mess with your mind. They will make you think every defeat is the termination of your mission. The distracters will trip you, then convince you your stumble is irrecoverable. When you stay on the ground, believing you can't get up, the distracters have sucked the vitality out of your emotional tank.

For Jesus, the cross was just the beginning. The sunset on Friday evening led to the sunrise of Sunday morning.

Don't let the distracters confuse your sunsets and sunrises.

Dealing with Distracters

Consider the Real Need of the Distracter

Mary's tears, costly perfume, and outpouring of passion for her deliverer may have been a distraction to Judas, but not Jesus. He saw the human being, not an intrusion.

Not all distracters are sinister plotters trying to steal your focus and drain your leadership reserves. Some are good people who are distracted themselves. They distract you only because they have lost their personal bearings. With such people, your mission as a leader is to help get them "undistracted."

That's what I (Shaun) had to do for Jake. Jake is one of the most talented, creative, witty guys I know. When I joined the Saddleback staff, he was responsible for programming. His wide range of talents contributed to effective, attractive events that reached many people. He handled logistics, calendaring, caterers, and decorations with efficiency. He was happy when people were reached through the special programs. Yet clearly he was not fulfilled or deeply joyful.

At first I feared it was something I had—or hadn't—done to help Jake. I took him aside to try to understand what was happening. As I got to know Jake, it became evident he was a shepherd, not a strategist. His heart beat for people, not programs.

Eventually an opening appeared on our staff roster for an evangelism pastor. I was given clearance from our human resources department to offer the spot to Jake. I arranged a meeting with him.

"Jake, I want to develop you as a pastor," I said. "We'd like you to take the evangelism pastor job that's opened up. We'll hire someone else for the programming position."

At first Jake was speechless. Then tears filled his eyes. "Man, I was burning out in the programming job. I've wanted to be a pastor so bad that I almost resigned. I wanted to tell you, but you seemed to really want me in the programming slot, so I kept quiet."

I realized that Jake was being distracted not because he was a slouch or mere adventurer but because he had a higher call.

Remember Why You're at the "Plate"

Yogi Berra was one of history's greatest distracters. As catcher for the New York Yankees, he would hack away with distracting words and sounds as opposing batters stepped up to the plate.

The Yankees met the Milwaukee Braves in a World Series. Hank Aaron, the Braves' star hitter, came up to bat. Yogi started immediately. "Henry, you're holding the bat wrong. You're supposed to hold it so you can read the trademark."

Aaron was silent. The next pitch zinged into the strike zone, and Aaron fired the ball into the left-field bleachers—a home run.

As he rounded the bases and stepped on home plate, Aaron turned to Yogi Berra. "I didn't come up here to read," he said.[4]

Occasionally, you must remind the distracters why you're here. "Hereness" in the deepest sense is treasuring the moment as sacred and a gift from God. It may be a hard moment, but even then it is to be honored as God-given.

At one point, for Daniel, "hereness" was a lions' den. But he treasured it as a split second when God could do something extraordinary in his life that would reveal the Lord to Daniel's Babylonian persecutors.

Unlike Daniel, many people lose sight of the value of the time and place God has assigned them. They languish in the "greener grass" syndrome, or the "more opportune time" phenomenon. Felix was one example. He was the Roman officer to whom Paul was brought when he was arrested toward the end of his ministry. Felix knew some things about Jesus' teachings. He and his wife asked Paul to come and explain more about Christ and his "Way."

> As [Paul] continued to argue about uprightness, purity of life (the control of the passions), and the judgment to come, Felix became alarmed and terrified and said, Go away for the present; when I have a convenient opportunity, I will send for you. At the same time he hoped to get money from Paul, for which reason he continued to send for him and was in his company and conversed with him often.
>
> Acts 24:25–26 AMP

Felix, like other Roman dignitaries, perhaps thought history would mark him for his valiant service to the Empire. Ironically, we remember Felix now only in relation to his prisoner, Paul.

For a special time, Felix had "hereness." Had he grasped the opportunity of those special moments, Felix's eternity would have been secured. But he was distracted by the fear of losing what his flesh craved and by his own desire to get money from Paul.

Don't let the distracters rob you of your "hereness." Treasure the times and places you have with family and friends. Freeze-frame special seasons and locations where you and those closest to you find unusual joy.

Your "amness" is another treasure the distracters will snatch from you if they can. "Amness" is what you are in Christ right now—not the wretch you were in past history or the spiritual giant you will be tomorrow. If you are in Christ, you are at this moment a "new creation," a Christlike man or woman, growing into the manifestation of his image already at work in you (see 2 Cor. 5:17). Christlike identity is your high vocation, your calling.

God gave you an identity, and he puts you in the place and role where you can best live out your true being in Christ. Above all else, don't let the distracters lure you away from that!

11

DIVERTERS

The diverters drain you through the constant pull to another path, set of values, vision, mission, goal, and strategy. They suggest their way will lead to your success quicker, or even to a better objective.

Diverters differ from the distracters in that the diverters believe theirs is the better course, while distracters are often merely curious, whimsical, and adventurous. Sometimes diverters are sinister.

At night on our small ranch in Texas, Irene and I (Wallace) can hear the wail of coyotes. When the shrill moan rides along the prairie, I think of the Jack London tales about the wolves in the far north. To seduce sled dogs, the wolves send a female to circle the sleeping Huskies. The big dogs pick up her scent and are tempted to leave the team and go chasing after the she-wolf, who leads them into the hungry, ferocious pack.

When my dog Charlie and I jog on our country road, rabbits are distracters to her, but, like the she-wolf, coyotes would be dangerous diverters.

Diverters and Their Diversions

In *Leadership on the Line*,[1] Harvard professors Ronald A. Heifetz and Marty Linsky write that the four basic dangers new leaders face are marginalization, diversion, attack, and seduction. All four can be elements of the same diversionary drain.

> What is common to all of these dangers is that they stem from a desire on the part of the group or community or organization to take you out of your game plan, to restore the status quo by shoving the difficult issue you are trying to surface back under the table where it cannot disturb anyone.[2]

To be marginalized is to be slowly edged out to the periphery, where you and your vision no longer seem to matter. Many a diversionary ploy aims at marginalizing leaders and their movements.

Every kid needs a parent to provide discipline and protection from diverters, every apprentice a master craftsman to point out departures from the blueprints, and every society a prophet to banner its truths continually so diversions will be spotted and avoided.

The church is to play the prophetic role in a nation. Powerful forces that want to divert a society to their vision will always try to marginalize the church. In China, the Communists tried to stamp it out, and when that failed, the authorities sought to push it out to the edge of society. The Nazis attempted to co-opt the church into an arm of its massive diversion of German intellect and energies. Some facets of the church bought into the diversionary schemes of Hitler and his team of tyrants, and those who didn't were marginalized and then, where possible, erased.

The schemes the diverters use to marginalize the church illustrate how the diversionary drain happens at all levels. Their plan employs alluring promises coupled with alluring tactics.

Alluring Promises

"We Will Give You Relevance"

The underlying implication is that you and your cause are meaningless in the contemporary consensus, which today is determined in many Western nations by four establishment elites: entertainment media, academia, news purveyors, and the political establishment. They promise if the church will embrace the consensus worldview, it will be regarded as "meaningful" to the public dialogue—which is usually a monologue by the elites.

The diversionary promise of relevance is a challenge to your values. The real message is this: "If you pull the plug on your values and embrace ours, we will regard you as relevant."

The trendy will always be snared by the promise of relevance. In working with high school youth, I (Shaun) see this tactic constantly. Some students get involved with our church because their parents insist on it. Such kids are easy to spot, because they are thoroughly acculturated with the contemporary worldview. They sit in Bible studies with a look on their face that reveals their thoughts: *You have nothing to say that is important to me and my lifestyle.*

It's vital to do all possible to reach such youth. In fact, it's a major thrust of our mission. But I have learned the moment we make ourselves "relevant" to them, we lose our true relevance as a prophetic voice.

Yes, communication styles and programming should be relevant, but this does not mean we compromise our values to reach students who have hooked into the culture's propaganda.

"We Will Give You a Place"

If the diverters can give you a "place," then they (and you) assume they own the real estate. Those in the United States, for example, who seek the marginalization of the church first spent much effort spreading the notion the country is in a "post-Christian" era.

The statistics would indicate otherwise if measured by church attendance. Though there may be some overestimation, regular church attendance in the United States has "rebounded to levels approaching the post-World War 2 period," especially among young adults and senior citizens.[3]

On July 2, 1795, the following notice appeared in a Baltimore newspaper:

> City of Washington, June 19. It is with much pleasure that we discover the rising consequence of our infant city. Public worship is now regularly administered at the Capitol, every Sunday morning, at 11 o'clock by the Reverend Mr. Ralph.

As writer David Barton points out, the cornerstone for the Capitol building was laid in 1793, but Congress didn't start meeting there until 1800. The United States Capitol was actually used as a church before the legislative body even moved in.[4] There is irony in the fact that politicians meeting in that building now embrace a policy that marginalizes the church.

The diversionary promise of a "place" is a challenge to your vision and mission. The diverters pull away from *your* vision and then "invite" you to have a part—usually peripheral—in contributing to *their* vision and mission. Gall is something diverters do not lack!

"We Will Give You a Voice"

The third alluring promise the diverters extend you is a "voice," a forum. Again, the cheekiness of the diverters is amazing. You probably gave them the forum from which they launched their movement. Now they promise to empower you if you will sing a new tune—theirs. The diversionary promise to give you a "voice" is a challenge to your message.

For example, the early church gave rise to the academic establishment, which now tries to limit the church's voice in the public square. Harvard University was founded in 1636 on property donated by the Reverend John Harvard, and it utilized his library. Its official mission was "to train a literate clergy." Yale was founded in 1701 by Congregational pastors "to propagate in this wilderness, the blessed Reformed, Protestant Religion, in ye purity of its order and worship." Princeton, known initially as the College of New Jersey, was launched by the Presbyterian Church in 1746 under the official motto "Under God's Power She Flourishes."[5]

The modern academic establishment in the United States has helped drain the country of its founding values by marginalizing the church. Tomes have poured from the Ivy League institutions suggesting the nation's founders intended a thoroughly secular society. Yet the elites who now control the institutions offer the church a "voice" if she will sing in their "choir"!

Alluring Tactics

Along with their alluring promises, the diverters will add alluring tactics.

Straight Line Backward

Diverters love history when they can twist it; otherwise they try to uproot it. One of their favorite schemes is to get you focused on an age they represent as "golden" and flatter you into thinking you're the one who can restore it. In the process, you forget the present and lose sight of the future. While you're wandering down Memory Lane, the diverters are stealing your organization and its team.

To avoid falling for the straight-line-backward ploy, know the flaws and mistakes of your predecessors and organization.

Straight Line Forward

The other extreme of the straight-line flimflam is to get you to ignite your rockets and blast off to a "gleaming" future.

You get out there with those future-seizing plans, throttled-up budgets, and fat blueprints and discover there is no one there with you. The diverters have led them up their road while you were zooming into orbit.

The hypervisioned leader is vulnerable to this subtle maneuver. Such a person is all heart and no head. Passions rule; excitement is easily stimulated.

To keep yourself from being set off like a moon rocket, consider your present resources and performance, then draw a well-reasoned plan for the future that no diverter can snatch from you.

Zigzag

This is among the craftiest of the diverters' alluring tactics. They compliment your present course, even seem to embrace it. Then suddenly the diverters invite you to come over and pick up enhancements.

Coca-Cola and Ford Motor Company both learned the costliness of the zigzag diversion. Coke replaced its classic drink with a new variety and found itself sinking in a sea of rejection. Ford had to quit producing the Edsel before the car crashed the whole company.

Coke and Ford were smart enough to zigzag again. The problem with many is once they've zigged, they find it hard to zag. Obviously, there is always room for improvement, so you must distinguish the diverters from the developers. Diverters are drainers; developers are energizers.

Sharp Left

Alluring tactic number four employed by the diverters is to try to "liberate" you from the "stifling" elements that give shape to your mission and visions.

For example, Hugh Hefner, creator of one of history's greatest diversionary scams, taught that traditional sexual mores are repressing people and making them neurotic, psychotic, and everything in between. Popular culture hopped merrily up this new path of thinking and found at its end the destruction of the family, the abortion holocaust, and the rampant spread of sexually transmitted diseases.

When the diverter invites you to smell the fresh wind of freedom, make sure your nostrils pick up the garbage odor as well.

Sharp Right

The sharp right alluring tactic used by diverters encourages you to turn your values into legalisms, your mission into a prescription, and your goals into regulations.

Sharp left wraps an anarchist's red bandanna around your head, but sharp right dresses you in a policeman's garb. Sharp left makes you an enabler rather than a leader, but sharp right casts you as a controller.

When the diverters urge you to take a sharp right, re-member leaders stay out front with sprinting shoes, not steel boots.

Jesus and the Diverters

Diverters surrounded Jesus, seeking to lure him away at five crucial points.

His Vision

A vision is a "preferred future." To understand Jesus' vision, consider the world before humanity's plunge into sin. Paradise was bounded with love, joy, and peace, made possible by four unities:

1. Adam was perfectly united to God.
2. Therefore, Adam was perfectly united to himself.
3. Therefore, Adam was perfectly united to other per-sons—the woman.
4. Therefore, Adam was perfectly united to nature.

The "preferred future" that energized Jesus' vision for the world was the reconciliation of all things to the Father. That relationship is foundational, and when it is restored, all other relationships harmonize.

The diverters, however, saw this as an impossible dream, a vision that had no hope of fulfillment. When they attacked him for forgiving sins, healing the sick, and casting out de-mons, they were calling for the status quo: leave the sinners in their guilt, the sick in their illnesses, and the demonized in their pathetic state.

It was sheer effrontery to the diverters for Jesus to sug-gest he could fulfill the vision of setting the upside-down world right side up!

His Values

For Jesus, grace always trumped law. He valued the Father's heart over the magistrate's gavel.

Pharisees were bothered by the Sadducees whom they considered anarchic, so they labored to fence in the law and then put the people behind the barricade. Jesus came to set people free. In the context of a synagogue in Nazareth during the first century AD, that freedom meant being loosed from the law.

The diverters tried continually to pull Jesus back onto the law road. They groused about him healing on the Sabbath. They muttered when his disciples didn't perform ceremonial washing. They were infuriated when he blithely forgave prostitutes and Roman soldiers and tax collectors.

But Jesus' heart never quit beating to the cadence of grace.

His Understanding of Himself

Jesus' enemies asked him one day in the heat of indignation, "Are you greater than our father Abraham, who died? Are you greater than the prophets, who died? Who do you think you are?" (John 8:53 NLT). He answered, "The truth is, I existed before Abraham was even born!" (John 8:58). Jaws dropped. Gasps whisked the air.

The diverters wanted to use theology and history—the straight-line-backward tactic—to pull Jesus away from his identity. But Jesus knew he was God's Son, and the Pharisees might as well have been trying to dislodge Mount Hermon.

His Strategy

Satan's third temptation of Jesus in the wilderness was aimed primarily at the Lord's strategy. The devil was too wise a diverter to try to turn Jesus from his vision, values, and understanding of himself. The adversary was smarter than the Pharisees.

Then the Devil took him to Jerusalem, to the highest point of the Temple, and said, "If you are the Son of God, jump off! For the Scriptures say, 'He orders his angels to protect you. And they will hold you with their hands to keep you from striking your foot on a stone.'" Jesus responded, "The Scriptures also say, 'Do not test the Lord your God.'"

Next the Devil took him to the peak of a very high mountain and showed him the nations of the world and all their glory. "I will give it all to you," he said, "if you will only kneel down and worship me."

"Get out of here, Satan," Jesus told him. "For the Scriptures say, 'You must worship the Lord your God; serve only him.'"

Matthew 4:5–10 NLT

Diverters are able to lure us away from our strategies when the end justifies the means. Satan was suggesting that Jesus should take the most expedient route to achieve his high goals. But the principles behind Jesus' strategy were as important as realizing his purpose. His goal would be compromised if he yielded to expediency.

His Destiny

The only way Jesus could realize his vision was to carry out his mission of giving his life "a ransom for many" (Mark 10:45). It's no surprise, then, that Jesus calls Simon Peter "Satan" when his friend unwittingly tries to divert him from his destiny.

It's Time for a Refill

When the diversion seems to be a better path.

"Broad is the road that leads to destruction," said Jesus (see Matt. 7:13). However, when you're exhausted from trying to see and press through the diversionary ploys, the easy, broad routes seem appealing.

I (Wallace) discovered that fact when a friend of mine was running for public office. An aide persuaded him to circulate an anonymous letter labeling his opponent as stupid and incompetent. Campaigning on the issues had been grueling, and the attack on the other candidate's mental faculties seemed an easier route to travel. In the end, my friend had to confess he penned the anonymous letter and apologize to the opponent and the public.

When you are diverted from your values and convictions.

Pastor Kevin strongly believed in the need for a restoration of moral values. He called sin "sin" and pointed out the traps sliding people into evil. His ministry soon grew beyond his one congregation. Television, books, and conferences all clambered for his attention and time.

No one knew the stressed, pressed pastor had been snared by a drug dealer. He was thoroughly drained, and in the desperation to get relief, Kevin separated from the values and convictions he preached and once held dear.

You're running on fumes when the diverters are able to move you away from the things you hold dearest.

Dealing with Diverters

Seek a Vision That Is Worth Dying For

You cannot be diverted from a vision for which you're willing to lay down your life.

Nothing could stop Jesus' three-year march toward Jerusalem and the cross. No theological meanderings could divert him from his Father's assignment. When the disciples talked about fire, Jesus thought of the "baptism of fire" he would soon undergo (see Luke 12:49–50). When his followers commented on the great stones of the temple complex, Jesus' focus was on his resurrection (see Matthew 24).

If your vision isn't worth dying for, it will seem not worth living for. But if your life and vision are one, you will not be diverted from your vision any more than you would lie down in front of a freight train!

Seek Values That Will Anchor You under the Diversionary Tides

A debate singes the American political landscape over the nature of the country's Constitution. "It is a *living* document," say those who want to adjust it to fit the values of the age. "Its principles are absolute and changeless," say those who value its rich truth.

Ideas, theories, suggestions, plans, and critiques of your own values will come and go like rippling tides, sometimes mounting to tsunami strength. If your values won't hold you steady, they are the wrong ones. Hollow values, like hollow anchors, provide no mooring.

Above all else, Jesus valued grace, and love is to grace what iron is to an anchor—its strength. No matter how strong the waves, he was immovable.

Seek a Mission That Will Make a Difference

Aleksandr Solzhenitsyn lived in a society where the state determined what truth was at a given moment. Truth was Solzhenitsyn's mission in the Communist-controlled Soviet Union. "One word of truth shall outweigh the whole world," he believed.[6]

The authorities sought to divert Solzhenitsyn by threats, imprisonment, and exile. But he knew his mission was transformational, and he wouldn't be drained of his passion for it. Missions that don't change things for the better are like plastic soldiers: they melt in the fire.

Embrace Attainable Goals

Hope in New Testament Greek means not an anticipation of what *might* be, but an expectation of what *will* be. "We have [this hope] as an anchor of the soul," says Hebrews 6:19.

If your goals are no more real than your anticipation of winning a national lottery, they won't stand the drain of the diverters. But when you can see the gold at the finish line, diverters cannot shift you from the goal of winning the race.

The diverters challenge the core of your identity, vision, mission, goals, and strategies. If that core is cheap, you will be easily pulled aside. But if it is the essence of your living in the present world, you are to the diverters what Gibraltar is to a thundering surf!

12

DOUBTERS

The doubters aren't convinced of you or your ability to execute the mission, and they drain you by influencing others with their doubt.

Cynics are *certain* your swan dive will be a belly flop. Doubters may be on your side but *lean toward* uncertainty that you have the capacity to execute a flawless dive.

The first drainer I (Shaun) met in my career was a doubter. As graduation neared, I looked for churches that might need a youth pastor. An elder at the church my dad served recommended me for the open position there.

However, my dad was hesitant. "Shaun, I would love for us to work together, but I don't think it will be best," Dad said. "There might be people who would think it's merely a father-son show."

I also was hesitant. The people in the congregation might see me more as the senior pastor's son than the youth pastor. I was concerned I would be judged not on my performance but by my last name. And if I failed, it could injure my dad's ministry.

Despite the objections, the elders pursued me. Their decision was unanimous except for one man, Luther. He had several objections I probably would have shared had I been sitting at his side of the table. First, he was concerned I was being considered only because I was the pastor's son. Second, he was troubled by the fact I was fresh out of college and inexperienced.

My dad supported me personally but backed away from the process, wanting to let the elders be free to decide. The elders had intense discussions with Luther, whose reservations about me persisted.

"Hiring Shaun would be a mistake," Luther said in one meeting. But the other elders disagreed with Luther, and the church called me as youth pastor. My first career assignment was one of the most difficult. I felt drained as I focused on convincing the doubter I was really up to the job.

Somewhere along the way my focus shifted from Luther to the Lord. I reconnected with why I was in ministry in the first place—not because of my dad, although I respected him, but because of God's call on my life and the passion he put in me for young people.

As my focus shifted, I forgot about looking at my backside to see who was watching me. I plowed forward, ministering to needy kids. And one day I heard miraculous words come out of Luther's mouth: "Shaun, I am so glad we called you as youth pastor. You are a tremendous asset to our team!"

The "Two Minds" of Doubt

The New Testament Greek word for *doubt* means "to be in two minds" or "to stand in two ways." The doubter drains you by convincing you assertion A is true, and then just as you are signing on to A, saying, "On the other hand, there's a lot of merit to B."

James reveals the draining effect of doubt when he writes, "A double minded man is unstable in all his ways" (James 1:8 KJV). Doubt wears you out, whether it's through an internal struggle or through the external doubters who make you wonder if your course is right.

Os Guinness, in his book *In Two Minds*,[1] says doubt should not be equated with unbelief. Neither should you assume if a person is in doubt he or she is tilting toward unbelief, the case of the cynic.

C. S. Lewis describes the dilemma: "Now that I am a Christian I do have moods in which the whole thing looks very improbable; but when I was an atheist I had moods in which Christianity looked terribly probable."[2]

My (Wallace) dog Charlie might not be on a par with Os Guinness and C. S. Lewis, but she understands well what it means to be "in two minds" and drained by doubt. When we got Charlie, a jet-black Labrador, I wanted a jogging partner and Irene wanted a leash dog. I would say "run" and Irene would say "heel." The dog practically was in need of psychotherapy. Doubts about her identity and place in our family were draining her.

So we got a leash and lap dog. Gillis is a small dog and loves to walk with Irene and sit in her lap in the den. Charlie's delight is running with me on country roads. Now that we have Gillis, Charlie is free to be who she is. She can be singularly focused.

The major reason the doubters drain your cause and team is because they are hesitant. You shout, "Charge!" and they ask, "Are you sure?"

Jesus and the Doubters

Thomas might be the patron saint of doubters—if they could be sure no one else is a better choice. But Thomas was not the only doubter. Doubting Jesus was an equal-opportunity profession. It consisted of snobby religious peacocks, uppity Roman soldiers, trembling members of his own family, and his sometimes reluctant team.

As Jesus' experience shows, doubters drain you with questions. Jesus faced more questions than a politician in a press conference. The questions posed to him shed light on how he handled the doubters.

Doubters Relish Rhetorical Questions

A rhetorical question enables the interrogator to make a point without being direct. It is a figure of speech through which a person makes a statement and to which they expect no answer. When Jesus is examined by Pontius Pilate, he begins talking about truth, and Pilate can respond only with a rhetorical question. Jesus says, "I have come into the world, to testify to the truth. Everyone who is of the truth hears My voice" (John 18:37). "What is truth?" Pilate asks rhetorically (v. 38).

Often when dealing with doubters, it's a temptation to want to score points. Sometimes that means taking the bait dangled by the rhetorical question, then attempting to respond or debate. Wisely, Jesus remains silent. Doubters aren't convinced by clever responses to unanswerable questions. Only relationship will dry up the doubt—and the rhetorical questions.

Doubters Thrive on Redundant Questions

Redundant questioning poses the same query in a different form each time. The problem with the redundant question is that rather than piercing through to an answer, it raises more doubt.

Here is a redundant line of questioning doubters hurled at or about Jesus: "By what authority are You doing these things?" (Matt. 21:23). "Who is the man who said to you, 'Pick up your pallet and walk'?" (John 5:12). "How does

He now say, 'I have come down out of heaven'?" (John 6:42).

Redundancy is like lava: it layers until it creates a mountain. In this case, the redundant questions spinning around Jesus' authority and divine origin become an alpine range, blocking faith.

Jesus shows a summary answer is the best response to redundant questioning. Such a response is a once-for-all assertion of the truth being questioned. The Lord's reply to the redundant questioning is in John 5:

> Truly, truly, I say to you, the Son can do nothing of Himself, unless it is something He sees the Father doing; for whatever the Father does, these things the Son also does in like manner. For the Father loves the Son, and shows Him all things that He Himself is doing; and the Father will show Him greater works than these, so that you will marvel. For just as the Father raises the dead and gives them life, even so the Son also gives life to whom He wishes. For not even the Father judges anyone, but He has given all judgment to the Son, so that all will honor the Son even as they honor the Father. He who does not honor the Son does not honor the Father who sent Him. Truly, truly, I say to you, he who hears My word, and believes Him who sent Me, has eternal life, and does not come into judgment, but has passed out of death into life. . . .
>
> I can do nothing on My own initiative. As I hear, I judge; and My judgment is just, because I do not seek My own will, but the will of Him who sent Me.
>
> verses 19–24, 30

Fully apply the brake of truth and the redundancy merry-go-round skids to a stop.

Doubters Collect Controversial Questions

Doubters hoard controversial questions like political junkies collect old campaign buttons. The hot-topic queries are often intended to reinforce doubt rather than rid people of it.

Some religious leaders said to Jesus one day, "Teacher, we know that You speak and teach correctly, and You are not partial to any, but teach the way of God in truth. Is it lawful for us to pay taxes to Caesar, or not?" (Luke 20:21–22).

Their aim was to skewer Jesus on a controversial question, reinforce the view that his aim was to overthrow the establishment, and shove the doubters deeper into skepticism about Jesus and his motives. But Jesus disarms them with his answer. He asks for a coin, notes it carries the image of Caesar, and says, "Give to Caesar what belongs to him. But everything that belongs to God must be given to God" (Luke 20:25 NLT).

The boom goes out of the controversy when the ammo is removed.

Doubters Get Snagged on Confusing Questions

Riddling questions hook doubters to their indecision: "How can there be evil if God is good?" "How can a good God send anybody to hell?" "Why do bad things happen to good people?"

"Who sinned, this man or his parents?" (John 9:2). That question was posed by Jesus' followers as they came across a blind man. Blindness is a disability; disabilities inflict sinners; therefore, either the man or his mother or father offended God. This was the confusing conundrum underlying the man's situation.

Doubters hang on a thread of uncertainty. Just as they decide to let go, a bothersome question snags them. It takes a sharp answer to snip the snag, such as the one Jesus gives: "It was not because of his sins or his parents' sins. . . . He was born blind so the power of God could be seen in him" (John 9:3 NLT).

Doubters Make a Game of Unresolved Questions

One winter day some temple-goers spot Jesus in the portico of the vast complex and ask him, "How long will You keep us in suspense? If You are the Christ, tell us plainly" (John 10:24). Jesus' answer shocks and offends them:

> I told you, and you do not believe; the works that I do in My Father's name, these testify of Me. But you do not believe because you are not of My sheep. My sheep hear My voice, and I know them, and they follow Me.
>
> John 10:25–27

Is Jesus being caustic and cold, rude and arrogant? Actually, Jesus sees through these doubters. They are able to pick him out of the temple mob in the first place because of his fame and notoriety. There should be no "suspense," because the works he has done ought to be enough evidence that he is the promised Messiah.

Jesus knows the doubters are toying with him and making a game of what is an unresolved question to them. He shows us that when those who doubt don't want resolution, arguing is pointless and only wastes time and energy.

It's Time for a Refill

When doubt blocks your view of the possibilities.

In my (Shaun) first job, which I described at the beginning of this chapter, the big threat from Luther the doubter was that I would become blinded to the possibilities of my new role. Day by day, week by week, I had to make sure Luther's blindness to my capabilities and what God could do through them didn't affect my vision of God and myself.

DOUBTERS

If you are losing sight of the wonderful opportunities in which God can use you, then the doubters are draining you. There are three things you must do to halt the drain.

Focus on God's bigness. Agree with your adversary quickly (see Matt. 5:25), even if he or she doubts you and your abilities. Say to the doubter outright or in your own inner discourse, "You're right; I'm too small for this job, but the God who put me here is bigger than the job, the organization, and the whole universe, so he's big enough to overcome my limitations!"

Focus on God's sovereignty. The first response includes an important point: if God put you in a role, he will supply what you need to accomplish the mission. I knew God himself had placed me in that first assignment and would give me any resources I lacked to do the job.

Focus on God's gifts. When the doubters suggest you don't have the talents for the task, remember you have God's gifts. Your talents may not measure up, but his gifts never fail. Your service is not through the adequacy of your natural abilities but through his supernatural enablement.

When you begin to feel like the Incredible Shrinking Man.

I (Wallace) am an old movie buff. "Honey," my wife said to me one night as we watched yet another black-and-white classic, "did you know they make movies in color now?"

One of my favorites is *The Incredible Shrinking Man*, made in 1957. Scott Carey is exposed to a mysterious mist and slowly shrinks down to microscopic size. Eventually he has to hide from his own cat and from spiders in the basement.

When you feel more like an amoeba than a giant with respect to your task and team, the doubters are draining you rapidly.

When the "maybes" lead you to "whatever."

When the doubters with their "maybe this" and "maybe that" attitude begin wearing out your reserves, your own outlook easily becomes the "whatever" mentality. This means you are wearying of dealing with the doubters—and everyone else.

The "whatever" makes you feel that your best efforts are worthless when the doubters are draining you.

When you map the exits before you enter a room.

Daniel's options in the lions' den were to trust God or map the exits before he entered.

If you have the exit strategies already mapped out when you face conflicts, the doubters have dipped deep into your emotional vitality. You might remember a time when you couldn't wait to take on a challenge, but doubt saps your confidence, and you're not sure you can hold up in the face of skepticism.

I (Wallace) discovered this when I ran for political office. Early on, I charged into debates, believing I could vanquish my opponents. As the campaign wore on, so did the opposition. Toward the end of the effort, I found myself wearying of the fight, and rather than eyeing the podium, I was searching for the exits.

I had to pull back, recover my vision and why I believed I was the best person for the office, and—above all—recover the strengths God had given me for political service. The podium got back into the center of my vision.

Dealing with Doubters

Make the Doubter Your Friend

Healthy relationship dries up doubt.

Luther became my (Shaun) friend. As he came to know me, he better understood my motives, ministry call, commitment, and potential. It was not only the way I did the job but also his discovery of my person that turned Luther into a supporter rather than a doubter.

In the meantime, I had the opportunity to discover who Luther was and better understand his concerns. Friendship opened up a trusting relationship, which led to the vulnerability of fellowship. In other words, I felt I could bare my heart's deepest desires to Luther with respect to our ministry. He could trust himself to me as well.

The cynic may be your foe, but give the doubter the benefit of the doubt. He or she may become your friend.

Make the Doubter Your Teammate

Jesus knew Thomas had a skeptical mind. Nevertheless, Jesus signed on Thomas as one of his disciples. He knew what he could do with this doubter.

Jesus didn't have our limitations. Sometimes we need the doubters on our team for what they can do for us as well as what we can do for them. You can turn the drain to gain by heeding their concern as fellow players and understanding how you can improve.

Make the Doubter Your Trusted Ally

Jesus told Simon Peter in advance that he would deny him. How long had Jesus known that? To answer that, we must look at Philippians 2:5–11. In his incarnation, Jesus laid down the perks of divinity, yet while he was fully human, he never ceased being fully divine. God has the attribute of foreknowledge. Therefore, Jesus always knew Peter would deny him.

Yet Jesus pulled Peter into his inner circle. This guaranteed a specific set of outcomes:

1. Peter would get over his doubts and repent of his denial.
2. Peter would become more committed than ever.
3. Peter would become a foundational person in the advance of the gospel.

Pulling a doubter into your inner circle is risky business. But a convinced, former doubter can become your greatest advocate.

Make the Doubter Your Cheerleader

The greatest advocate of all is a cheerleader. Even Thomas, the poster child of the doubters, became Jesus' cheerleader. Tradition says Thomas wound up ultimately in India, dying a horrible death for the Lord about whom he had once voiced his doubts.

In dealing with Luther—who became a cheerleader for me (Shaun)—I had to get my eyes off the doubter and onto God and the mission to which he had sovereignly called me.

I didn't focus on making Luther my cheerleader; instead I gave my all to the task of ministering to our youth. When he saw the results, Luther became my cheerleader.

No one shows how to turn a doubter into a cheerleader like Jesus. Thomas had declared that if he saw Jesus' pierced hands and side he would believe in the resurrection. When Jesus appeared to him and the other disciples, the Lord invited Thomas to inspect his wounds.

Your doubters will become convinced when they see your scars. Your wounds, not your words, make them your cheerleaders.

The antidote to doubt is credibility. Some of the British doubted the credibility, motives, and methods of St. Patrick, the great missionary who opened barbaric Ireland to the gospel. "He went to Ireland to con riches from the guileless Irish—haven't you heard he charges for baptisms and bishoprics? Did you know that he was a swineherd to begin with, a filthy little pigkeeper?"[3]

Yet in the end, the people who doubted Patrick became his followers, friends, allies, and cheerleaders. Ultimately Patrick became the hero of Ireland. The doubters were transformed as they watched him minister and heard him teach.

Get your mind off the doubters and their draining uncertainty, get on task, and let God work through you.

The cynics may never be convinced, but the doubters will!

13

EXASPERATORS

We classify exasperators as T-type (Tormentors) and D-type (Duh). D-types suck the life from you because they don't "get it." T-types "get it" but are too stubborn to do anything about it.

Ignore the "Ts" because they only want to drain you. Encourage the "Ds" because eventually they will "get it."

Encounter with "Tormentor"

Teresa and I (Shaun) had bought our kids a funtube at our local megamart. A funtube is a foamy float that costs five bucks and lasts about an hour in an average child-thrashed swimming pool. We sat in deck chairs at our neighborhood pool, pretended we were on a Mediterranean cruise, and watched our kids play. There was a seven- or eight-year-old kid who was torturing everyone in his theater of war.

"Tormentor" was playing with his own purple funtube. Actually, he seemed to be eating it. Flecks of foam clung to his jowls. However, I realized he was not swallowing the foam when he spit a purple slice of it at another kid.

"Tormentor" moved in our direction. Our fleet went on alert as he walked straight to our son's funtube lying next to Teresa and me and grabbed it.

"Excuse me, that's my son's funtube," said Teresa.

"No, this is mine!" shrieked the exasperator.

"It can't be," my wife replied, "because your funtube has big chunks from where you bit it."

That gave "Tormentor" a creative idea for pushing exasperation to new limits. He chomped down on our son's funtube and spit the foam pieces at my wife.

Now, Teresa had attended the Air Force Academy and spent nine years defending her country before retiring as an Air Force captain. But all she could do against "Tormentor" was hop up in her exasperation and say to our kids and me, "Let's go before I lose control!"

Normally we arrived home from the neighborhood pool refreshed. On that day we were drained by our exasperating encounter with "Tormentor."

Somebody in your home, church, school, or workplace probably has the name "Tormentor." There may be whole families of them in your world. They invent ways to prod you into rage or insanity. They have heads as thick as granite. Toss them pearls and they grind them into the grit.

An hour with an exasperating tormentor leaves you limp.

Jesus and the Exasperators

In Jesus' daily routine, the scribes, Pharisees, and Sadducees were usually of the T-type, but the disciples sometimes fell into the D-type.

"Tormentors" are determined to snatch your soul through their stubbornness, but "Duhs" wear you down with "dumbness." Explain it to them, draw them pictures, show them the equations, or build them a model, and they just sit there with their mouths drooping and say, "Duh."

Just after Jesus fed a crowd of four thousand on a few morsels of bread and fish, he faced both types of exasperators. The T-types "came out and started in on him, badgering him to prove himself, pushing him up against the wall" (Mark 8:11 Message).

The Bible says Jesus was "sighing deeply in His spirit" (v. 12). This was more than breathing. The original Greek term indicates the Lord was groaning. If you've ever given an exasperated sigh or groaned as if to say, "Good grief!" you get the idea.

Exasperation is not a sin. We know that because Jesus was exasperated with the Pharisees: "Why does this generation clamor for miraculous guarantees? If I have anything to say about it, you'll not get so much as a hint of a guarantee" (v. 12 Message).

With the T-type still on his mind, Jesus linked up with his disciples, who were grousing because somebody forgot to pack lunch. They were Team Duh, forgetting that earlier in the day they had watched their Master feed four thousand people on seven loaves of bread and a few small fish.

"Why are you fussing because you forgot bread?" Jesus asked the D-types. "Don't you see the point of all this? Don't you get it at all? Remember the five loaves I broke for the five thousand? How many baskets of leftovers did you pick up?"

"Twelve," muttered a "Duh."

"And the seven loaves for the four thousand—how many bags full of leftovers did you get?"

"Seven," mumbled another "Duh."

Jesus looked at them, maybe amazed at their thickheadedness. "Do you still not get it?" he asked (see Mark 8:17–21 Message).

But eventually they did, which is why you don't want to give up on the D-type exasperators. In fact, the key to turning the drain to gain in relationships with exasperators is to discern the type.

It's Time for a Refill

When your sighs turn to snorts.

There are stages of exasperation. First is the sigh of mild frustration. If the exasperator continues the drain, the sigh mutates into a furious snort.

Dealing with T-Type Exasperators

Jesus gives some clues for relating to the T-type exasperators who torment you to the edge of sanity.

Don't Let Them Put Stumbling Blocks in Your Path

The scribes, Pharisees, and Sadducees were out to exasperate Jesus, but a good bit of the time he exasperated them. They wanted to snatch his soul, but he wanted to give them a new one.

There was the day they wanted to snare Jesus with the question about paying taxes. The Pharisees teamed up with the Herodians to try to trip Jesus. They were like Republicans and Democrats agreeing on a common agenda. The Pharisees regarded the Herodians as compromisers to the corrupt culture, and the Herodians considered the Pharisees a bunch of religious stuffed shirts. But they agreed on one thing: their desire to stop Jesus.

So they brewed up a scheme. "Is it lawful to give a poll-tax to Caesar, or not?" (Matt. 22:17). They put the question to Jesus in front of a whole bunch of people. If Jesus answered the question one way, he would appear to the crowd to be aligning with the Romans. If he responded with another answer, he could be guilty of treason.

Instead, Jesus refused to be lured into an argument. He asked for a coin, reminded them of Caesar's face on its surface, and replied with his famous line, "Render to Caesar the things that are Caesar's; and to God the things that are God's" (v. 21).

The Bible says these T-type soul snatchers walked away "amazed" (v. 22). The original Greek word for *amazed* means "wonder" and "admiration." Later events will show that the T-type exasperators who dogged Jesus' every step admired his ability to outwit them, but doing so increased their own exasperation at being unable to slow him down.

Don't Try to Reason with Them Until They Are Ready

The Pharisees were the right-wing religious zealots, the Herodians the pragmatic political centrists, and the Sadducees the theological left wing. They all were T-type exasperators.

Not long after Jesus refused to fall into the poll-tax trap, the Sadducees tried to snare him. They approached Jesus with a complex question about marriage and whom a multiple-wedded woman would belong to in the resurrection. These soul snatchers were asking about something that would happen in the resurrection when they didn't even believe there would be one!

Rather than trying to reason and debate with these T-types about the doctrine of resurrection, Jesus headed straight to the point. "The reason you are mistaken [is] that you do not understand the Scriptures or the power of God" (Mark 12:24).

Reason gets you nowhere with a "Tormentor" who tries to drain your very soul. That day at the pool, Teresa tried to reason with "Tormentor" by pointing out he had the wrong funtube. She was right in leaving. She withdrew before he exasperated her so much she lost control.

Be Prepared to Take Advantage of an Opportune Moment

Ignoring T-types means you turn away from their obnoxious, obstructing behavior for the moment. But Jesus' style of connecting with people meant he kept watching for opportunities to touch even the T-types.

Nicodemus apparently didn't act like all the other Pharisees, but he belonged to the class. Nevertheless, Jesus was ready to sit and converse with Nicodemus when he was ready to listen.

And there were others transformed from T-type exasperators to committed disciples. "Many even of the rulers believed in Him" (John 12:42). The "rulers" were members of the Sanhedrin, the Supreme Court of Judaism—men like Nicodemus and Joseph of Arimathea.

The strategy with the T-type exasperators is to ignore them when they're trying to block your progress and crush your dreams but be ready to reach out to them when they soften.

For example, among your T-types there may be a Saul of Tarsus. This tormentor delighted in exasperating the followers of Christ. He tormented them with terror and drained them with his threats. But all along, the Lord of heaven had his eyes on this "Pharisee of the Pharisees."

There came a day when Saul was on his way to Damascus to carry out a raid on the church there. But Jesus knew this was Saul's day to change. And the Pharisee became a disciple like no other. The T-type exasperator was changed into a top-rate follower of Jesus.

Don't Ever Stop Caring about Them

Jerusalem was a city full of T-type exasperators. They clustered at the temple. One day some of them came out to meet Jesus as he approached Jerusalem. They warned Jesus not to go to Jerusalem, telling him Herod wanted him dead.

Jesus refused to let the T-types block his journey. But his compassion for them burst into the open as he said, "O Jerusalem, Jerusalem, the city that kills the prophets and stones those sent to her! How often I wanted to gather your children together, just as a hen gathers her brood under her wings, and you would not have it!" (Luke 13:31).

Dealing with D-Type Exasperators

The D-type exasperators, like the muddled confusers in chapter 4, require skill and finesse as well. While you may never reach the tormentors, there's a much greater chance of developing a gaining relationship with the D-types. Some of the T-types' minds are so closed that not even the Jaws of Life could pry them open. But the D-types have doors that have keyholes. Find the key that fits, and a draining relationship of exasperation is turned into a gaining relationship of aspiration, commitment, and fulfillment.

Don't Give Up on Them

On the last leg of his earthly journey, Jesus traveled to Jerusalem. The route led through Samaria, where people in some of the villages refused to accommodate Jesus and the disciples.

James and John were snorting over the snub. "Lord, do You want us to command fire to come down from heaven and consume them?" (Luke 9:54).

"Of course not," the Lord replied. He let them know they were clueless by reminding them he hadn't come to kill people but to give them life.

"What losers!" might be the twenty-first-century evalua-
tion, but not Jesus'. Though James and John's ignorance of
his fundamental mission—even after following him three
years—was exasperating, Jesus did not give up on them.
And history records that these "Duh" brothers went on to
be among the most valiant of Jesus' disciples.

Encourage Them

On another day the D-team was acting the part, fussing over who was the greatest. They had heard Jesus'
teachings about the meek, humble, and small. They had
listened to his bottom-up gospel. Their arguing over being
the top dog showed how thickheaded and exasperating
they were.

Maybe Jesus saw Simon Peter strutting or smirking as if
to say, "It's a no-brainer; everybody knows I'm the disciple
with a capital *D*!" Whatever the case, as Jesus was straight-
ening out the disciples about the concept of greatness, he
turned suddenly and looked at Peter.

> Simon, stay on your toes. Satan has tried his best to sepa-
> rate all of you from me, like chaff from wheat. Simon, I've
> prayed for you in particular that you not give in or give
> out. When you have come through the time of testing, turn
> to your companions and give them a fresh start.
>
> Luke 22:31–32 Message

In one breath, Jesus both warned and encouraged
Simon "Duh" Peter. The fisherman who would one day
write powerful letters that would influence millions of
people had no inkling of what Jesus was saying at the
moment.

But his Master was encouraging Peter. The disciple was
going to be tested, but he was going to make it through
successfully, and with such victory he would be in a position to inspire and motivate his pals.

Once You Win Their Hearts, Connect with Their Heads

In response to Jesus' statement, Peter sputtered, "Master, I'm ready for anything with you. I'd go to jail for you. I'd die for you!" (Luke 22:33 Message).

Jesus perhaps looked piercingly into Peter's eyes. "I'm sorry to have to tell you this, Peter, but before the rooster crows you will have three times denied that you know me" (v. 34 Message).

There comes a moment in your interactions with the D-type when it's time for the facts. The heart is the route to the head.

In a church I (Shaun) served as youth pastor, the facilities manager griped constantly about teens messing up his buildings. For months, he really worked at being the pebble in my shoe. He griped and griped, and I became angrier and angrier. He would drive at me, and I would hammer at him. I would always leave those confrontations exasperated and drained, pouting and murmuring in my frustration, and wishing the clash had never happened.

The morning after one of the worst of these blow-ups I was reading Jesus' words in Luke 6:

> But I say to you who hear, love your enemies, do good to those who hate you, bless those who curse you, pray for those who mistreat you. Whoever hits you on the cheek, offer him the other also; and whoever takes away your coat, do not withhold your shirt from him either. Give to everyone who asks of you, and whoever takes away what is yours, do not demand it back. Treat others the same way you want them to treat you. If you love those who love you, what credit is that to you? For even sinners love those who love them. If you do good to those who do good to you, what credit is that to you? For even sinners do the same. If you lend to those from whom you expect to receive, what credit is that to you? Even sinners lend to sinners in order to receive back the same amount. But love your enemies, and do good, and lend, expecting

nothing in return; and your reward will be great, and you will be sons of the Most High; for He Himself is kind to ungrateful and evil men. Be merciful, just as your Father is merciful.

Luke 6:27–36

I realized I had become brittle with exasperation at "Brother Duh." The Lord's words were like an air hammer, breaking the shell I had cemented around myself to stop the drain every time "Brother Duh" showed up. I prayed God would help me develop a positive relationship with this exasperating drainer. I promised myself that when he came with a complaint, I would respond with an apology and a specific word of encouragement.

It didn't take long for the new strategy to be put to the test. Into my office came "Brother Duh" with his latest lament over our youth.

My hackles went up, and all I wanted to do was defend our ministry and the kids. Instead I said, "I'm really sorry. I know you work hard to keep everything clean and working right, and I really appreciate what you do."

My stomach knotted that first time, and I felt like a groveling idiot. But I was determined to follow Jesus' directions for dealing with this type of exasperator. After another month, the tension in my stomach started easing when I saw "Brother Duh" coming. And I noticed his negative comments were fading.

Eventually "Brother Duh" turned into "Brother Bud." Our relationship grew, and he became one of the hardest-working volunteers in our youth ministry. The exasperator was transformed into one of the most loyal, passionate, and helpful team members I've ever had.

Never give up on the exasperators. Figure out which category they're in. Encourage the D-types to get on the team. Ignore the T-types when they're trying to block the path, but be ready to bring them in when they're ready.

And always walk into relationships concerning exasperators of both types with faith-fired confidence. Even draining interactions with tormentors can be transformed into gainful relationships if you're willing to connect Jesus-style.

14

FOOT DRAGGERS

Foot draggers drain you by pulling back just when you are trying to lead forward. I (Shaun) learned about foot draggers while working with a talented young lady I will call Morticia for reasons you'll soon understand.

Morticia rotated every few weeks as our volunteer worship leader. Her music sounded like it had been composed in a Romanian castle by a zombie hunched over an ancient, dusty organ. Every time she was in charge, we could have draped the room in black crepe.

A jokester once said that when Brahms was in a really light mood he would compose music with the theme "the grave is my joy." Morticia could have sung the tune from memory.

"This is a high-energy service," I explained to her one day. "You're dragging us down by opening with such slow, heavy music."

"No," she replied. "When I lead worship, that's the kind of music I think we ought to use to get things started."

Started where? I wondered. *The local morgue?*

"Look, I agree we ought to have a mix of music," I explained. I didn't think it should all be a Gregorian chant set in a minor key.

However, Morticia had her agenda, and it seemed nothing would change it. Morticia was a valuable member of our team, and we wanted and needed her, but she was dragging us down.

Jesus and the Foot Draggers

Jesus faced foot draggers every day. His message and call were radical. Once as he was surrounded with yet another mob, there seemed to be a hint of a breakthrough. "Teacher, I will follow You wherever You go," said a scribe (Matt. 8:19).

Jesus responded, "Okay, but you need to know that even though foxes have holes in the ground where they can sleep and the birds have their nests, I, the Son of Man, don't have a house to go home to at night" (v. 20 authors' paraphrase).

Another follower scampered up. "Before I can go along with you I have to go home and wait for my elderly father to die so I can be around to bury him" (v. 21 authors' paraphrase).

Foot draggers were all around Jesus. But he knew how to turn them into sprinters, charging ahead with the mission.

I hate to pick on Simon Peter, but he did set himself up as a hefty target. More than once he showed his feet crawled with the foot-dragging bug. Even after the crucifixion, resurrection, ascension, and Pentecost, occasionally he was still returning to some of his old ideas and religious practices.

There was, after all, that episode in Antioch when he refused to eat with Gentile Christians after some Jews showed up. He feared the Jews would paste him with the same "unclean" label they stuck on the Gentiles (see Gal. 2:11–14). Peter seemed to be shouting, "Retreat! Back to Judaism!" And this was after the Holy Spirit had shown him in a dream there was no one "unclean" in God's eyes (see Acts 10:9–16)! Yet here Peter was dragging his foot in the dirt, unwittingly trying to slow the momentum of the gospel into the non-Jewish world.

What motivated this guy to get on Jesus' team in the first place?

Years earlier Jesus had encountered Peter on the beach with his brother, Andrew. "And he said to them, 'Follow Me, and I will make you fishers of men'" (Matt. 4:19). Quick as a trout swallows a fly, "they left their nets and followed Him" (v. 20).

Simon Peter was no foot dragger that day!

It's Time for a Refill

When the weight on the end of your chain is a living being.

Recently I (Wallace) tried to jog with my wife's small dog, Gillis. I attached him to a leash and set off along the track. The little dog's stubby legs wouldn't keep up. My whole pace changed as the living being on the end of the chain dragged behind. I returned from the run drained rather than energized. Similarly, foot draggers slow your pace.

When it seems your whole day was filmed in slow motion.

When you go home at night wishing someone would speed up the camera, you have probably spent much time with foot draggers. Your tank is running dry when the walk up your driveway feels like a nightmare in which your legs are stuck in concrete as a monster closes in.

Dealing with Foot Draggers

Jesus' secret was in discovering a person's "I-zone," the chunk of humanity in all of us that responds to inspiration and ignites our passion. Press that spot, and we are motivated to pull up anchors, let go of the brakes, and leave our nets, even if we are world-class foot draggers.

Knowing the characteristics of the I-zone will help you identify the point of inspiration in the foot draggers inhabiting your world.

Characteristic 1

The I-zone is the task, relationship, or place corresponding to a person's deepest-held values.

Winston Churchill and Franklin Roosevelt faced a Parliament, a Congress, and two nations full of foot draggers as World War II brewed. Churchill, as a member of Parliament, pled with his colleagues to take the German threat seriously and get Great Britain on a war footing. By the time the Battle of Britain seared the landscape and skies in 1940, the British barely had enough planes to meet the Nazi bomber flocks.

In the United States, President Roosevelt was having a hard time motivating the Congress and much of the public to understand the seriousness of the Nazis' grim plans.

Churchill gave a clue to his own determination to inspire Britain to stand up to the Germans. On June 18, 1940, after the fall of France to Hitler, Churchill told the British people he expected the battle for Britain to begin soon. In words that put fire into the foot draggers, Churchill said,

> Upon this battle depends the survival of Christian civilization. . . . But if we fail, then the whole world, including the United States, including all that we have known and cared for, will sink into the abyss of a new Dark Age made

more sinister, and perhaps more protracted, by the lights of perverted science.[1]

Churchill drove for the I-zone of the Western world by appealing to its deepest values, and he inspired even the most ponderous foot draggers to get on the team to defeat the Nazis.

Characteristic 2

The I-zone is the task, relationship, or place where a person feels the most confident.

To learn how to connect with foot draggers Jesus-style, look again at the exchange between Jesus and Simon Peter. Imagine if the conversation had gone something like this:

"Greetings, guys," says Jesus. Then the Lord looks at Peter as he's busy swirling his fishing net through the Sea of Galilee. "Come with me because I want to teach you how to preach sermons that'll wrench the hearts out of the Pharisees and write history-shaking theological treatises."

"You've got the wrong guy," the fisherman responds.

But that wasn't how the Lord did it. Matthew 4:18 says when Jesus walked up, Peter and Andrew were casting their nets into the sea *because they were fishermen.* Jesus appealed to their identity, their self-perception, their heartbeat—which was fishing. "I will make you fishers of men," Jesus said (v. 19). Now that was an invitation that appealed to Peter.

You'll know when you touch a foot dragger's I-zone. In words, actions, or both, he or she will let you know, "I can do this!"

So to inspire the foot draggers, develop a caring relationship that will lead you to discover the place where they perform so well that they forget all the reasons the big plan won't work. A sharp lady we'll call Dorenda shows how.

She answered her phone one day and couldn't believe what she heard. Talking on a speakerphone were her pastor and the chairman of the huge building project her church was undertaking. Why would these two powerful men phone her?

"Dorenda, we have a big job for you," said the pastor.

"And we're really praying you'll take it on, because you're perfect for it," chimed in the chairman.

"As you know," the pastor continued, "the worship auditorium we're building will be state of the art. We want the decor to match the technological excellence."

Dorenda gulped. She knew nothing about technology.

The chairman spoke. "Our building committee is unanimous that you are the best organizer any of us know and that you have a real eye for decorating."

"We want you to serve as chair of the interior design subcommittee," the pastor said.

Dorenda's heart sped up and her blood flow quickened. In her soul, Dorenda knew she was made for exactly this kind of assignment, one that would combine her leadership skills with her love for beauty.

Within a week Dorenda assembled her subcommittee. Among the people she picked was Cheryl, whose reputation for being a hard worker was known throughout the church.

"I'm not sure I should do this," said Cheryl when Dorenda sought to recruit her.

"Is it your personal schedule?" Dorenda asked. "We can find ways to work around that."

"No," replied Cheryl, gazing down at the floor. "To tell you the truth, I think our church is going overboard with this building project. It's too expensive for us."

Dorenda was amazed and disappointed. She needed not only Cheryl's commitment to hard work but her influence as well. Dorenda quietly scolded herself for trying to recruit Cheryl when she didn't even know her. She realized she needed to connect with Cheryl as a person rather than merely try to pull her onto a subcommittee.

Dorenda went to Cheryl's house to talk and found herself studying the living room, where she and Cheryl sat. Its colors flowed like a work of art. The tones exuded peace, security, reassurance, and joy. Dorenda didn't want to leave. She realized this was exactly what the colors of the new sanctuary should accomplish.

"Thanks for being honest with me about the building project," Dorenda said. "Why don't we get together and talk some more about your concerns? I'd be happy to spend some time with you to understand your point of view."

Over the next month, Dorenda met weekly with Cheryl. They went to lunch, met at a mall and window shopped, and sat down for coffee. Finally Dorenda said, "I know you're not enthusiastic about the building program, but that decision has already been made, and it isn't going to change. I have a huge challenge in organizing the plan for decorating the new auditorium, but I know almost nothing about coordinating colors. You have a great eye for color. If you feel you couldn't serve on the subcommittee, would you consider being a private consultant to me on the color scheme?"

Cheryl brightened. Color? Few things excited her more. "I would love that!" she said.

Dorenda had connected with Cheryl's I-zone, the place where this foot dragger became inspired to play a role in a project she wasn't sure about. Ultimately Cheryl became one of the greatest fans of the new building.

Characteristic 3

The I-zone is the task, relationship, or place in which an individual finds greatest compatibility with his or her spiritual gifts and personality type.

Personality is the spandex of spiritual gifts. Without meaning to trivialize sacred things, here's the way it all works, according to God's Word: the spiritual gifts God gives us enable us to carry out the purposes for which we were put in the world, and our personalities are designed to keep those gifts in line with his knowledge of our purpose.

Here's an example: if you tour England's Windsor Castle, you will trek through the armor room. The metalware in which King Henry VIII dressed his bulky body is there. If you've seen his portrait, the armor doesn't have to be labeled. You would know it was designed for Henry VIII because the metal suit has a protruding stomach. Similarly, your personality is shaped to fit your spiritual gifts.

I (Shaun) found this out when someone's granny came to me one day and said she wanted to join our student ministries volunteer staff. I shuddered to think of all the foot dragging she could bring. When I told my staff about Granny wanting to link up with us, the jokes flew.

Granny blunted our barbed humor not by what she said but by what she did. I had mentioned to her that our junior high kids came to church like a school of sharks in a feeding frenzy. Granny hopped right in there. "I'll bring some snacks," she said. Think of a Sunday brunch at Bill Gates's country club. Croissants, home-baked bread, fresh fruit, and other morsels were piled on tables outside the junior high meeting room.

Best of all, the blue-haired lady became a friend to some of those kids. Students who knew maybe one parent besides their own now had a granny in their lives. Week after week she brought in eats that would knock your socks off, and she loved on kids who lapped up the attention while they downed her fresh-made snacks.

The lady I was sure would be a foot dragger proved to be an out-front runner. The reason was Granny had spiritual gifts of shepherding and hospitality. Her personality pulsated. Probably her well-used joints didn't even creak.

Granny was in her I-zone and didn't have time to be "elderly"!

Characteristic 4

The I-zone is the task, relationship, or place that meshes perfectly with a person's perceived mission in life.

This understanding is what transformed Morticia into a Mary Magdalene—an exuberant, passionate, even zesty leader.

One day it hit me (Shaun) that the problem wasn't this young woman; it was her leadership—namely, me. Whether you're a parent, manager in a company, pastor, school teacher, coach, or CEO, when those you want to follow you are dragging their feet, begin by looking at yourself as the leader.

When I began thinking that way, I realized I had neglected to relate the big picture to Morticia. Through a series of conversations I described the purpose of the particular service in which she helped lead worship. One day a light bulb popped on and illuminated the whole plan and her place in it.

It turned out the lady's mission in life was to lead people into an encounter with God through worship. When she saw her crucial role in our gatherings, she understood how all the pieces of the puzzle came together. Until then she had been a separate entity, somebody who was slapped into a hole in the puzzle but had no idea how her mission contributed to the whole. When she grasped the fact her taste in music was obstructing fulfillment of her mission, Miss Foot Dragger became Miss Praise Leader, which is what she had always wanted to be.

The next time she led worship, God used her to electrify the students. We soared to the heights and explored the depths of praise. The foot dragger got out front because she connected her personal mission to the whole enterprise.

Characteristic 5

The I-zone is the task, relationship, or place in which one's dreams have the greatest potential of coming true.

Foot draggers tend to be quiet, cautious people. Usually we assume their rare dreams are all in black and white and are no more exotic than envisioning new grout for the shower.

Wrong.

Foot draggers can be big dreamers. But often they fear disappointment, so they shut down the dream as fast as your mother turned off the TV when something racy shot before your eyes. Get a foot dragger into a situation where her dreams can become reality, and you have a person who can outdash the Road Runner.

Janice was a notorious foot dragger. The momentum she slowed was that of her own destiny. At twenty, Janice was at a crossroads. She was an on-again, off-again collegian. In two years she had switched majors twice. Now she was off for a semester, working at a fast-food restaurant.

"Janice, your problem is you have no ambition," said her hyperactive sister, Barbara. Janice's sibling, a year and a half older, was already clerking at a law firm and dreaming of being the first female chief justice of the U.S. Supreme Court.

Meanwhile, Janice languished in the backwaters.

Neither Barbara nor anyone else in Janice's life knew the enormity of her dreams. Janice wanted to sing opera. She yearned to make tones so piercing they would shatter stage lights. Janice dreamed of dancing across the stage of New York's Metropolitan Opera, garbed in a bright, flowing gypsy skirt as she sang the lead role in *Carmen*.

When Janice had dared expose a small corner of her dream to her unlettered father, he snapped, "You need to think about getting a *real* job."

So Janice had majored in education, thinking perhaps she could be a schoolteacher. Her interest was as flat as the desert floor. She switched to business. Maybe she could work up an aspiration to be General Motors's CEO. Or secretary. The desert turned into Death Valley.

She was tired of changing majors and dropped out of college.

Then one Sunday Janice was asked to solo with the choir at church. She had given up on herself and usually looked frumpy. But she was so excited about singing, her whole countenance changed. She dressed herself up and, with uncharacteristic excitement, hurried to church.

Afterward Janice's dad walked toward her as he dabbed his eyes with a handkerchief. "Honey, that was the most beautiful thing I ever heard," he sniffed.

Her father's words healed Janice's leaden feet. The next morning she contacted the music school she had wanted to attend desperately. The school was expensive, and Janice would have to hold down a job while pursuing her operatic ambitions.

But it didn't matter. Janice could now see the top of the mountain. She knew her dreams could become reality, and her foot-dragging days ended right there.

Expulsive Power

Thomas Chalmers, a nineteenth-century preacher in Scotland, spoke of "The Expulsive Power of a New Affection." You can try to scare foot draggers into moving, light firecrackers under their feet, hook a chain around their neck, or attempt to pull them forward, but none of it works. But when foot draggers are ignited by a fresh love, a newly awakened passion, or a revived hope, no one can outrun them!

That's what it means to discover their I-zone. The discovery requires you take time to know the foot draggers in your midst. Rather than writing them off, build a relationship.

Who knows? You may have a Morticia struggling to become a Mary Magdalene, a granny wanting to be a godmother, or perhaps even a Simon yearning to be a Rocky (see Matt. 16:18).

15

FREELOADERS

Freeloaders are drainers who hop onto your bandwagon only for the ride, contributing nothing to the journey. They are with you strictly for what they can get out of it, which frequently is a great deal.

"We've all worked with folks who accept the rewards but contribute little to group tasks, hence the label 'freeloader,'" writes leadership expert Christopher M. Avery. The freeloader attitude, he says, "costs everyone—sometimes a lot more than we want to admit."[1]

It was hard to admit I (Shaun) was a draining freeloader. As a college freshman, I was an hour from my parents' house, so every weekend I would scamper there like a puppy. My mother cooked up luscious meals and washed my clothes, and she and my dad made me feel warm and loved. They didn't even require quarters to do my laundry.

I started bringing pals home for the weekend, first one, then a couple. When we left, the pantry looked like a cotton patch after a boll weevil convention. Sometimes when we had stripped the house bare, Mom and Dad would take my guests and me out to dinner. You can guess who paid the whole tab.

One day not long ago my mom made a shocking confession: those weekends at home with my friends were an immense drain on her and Dad. I had the illusion their funds were limitless, but the reality was they struggled to pay the bills.

"Why didn't you tell me how much it was hurting you?" I asked her.

She smiled. "Shaun, it was all worth it to have you come home for the weekend."

"Freddie the Freeloader" Is Everywhere

Red Skelton made the character "Freddie the Freeloader" famous. The draining freeloader spirit is everywhere.

Some Politicians Aim to Drain the Barrel Dry

Many—if not most—elected officials sincerely desire to serve the public. In fact, public service is costly, demanding sacrifice. But there are scoundrels who expect a payback.

Few have been as blatant as California congressman Randall "Duke" Cunningham. When it came to being a draining freeloader, the prosecutors in his case said they could think of no other parallel in U.S. Congress history.[2]

Cunningham even had a "bribery menu" sporting the seal of the United States Congress. For every one million dollars he acquired for contractors from the government, Cunningham expected fifty thousand dollars for himself.

In the end, the drain was greater than the surge. "I broke the law, concealed my conduct and disgraced my office," said Cunningham. "I know that I will forfeit my freedom, my reputation, my worldly possessions, [and] most importantly, the trust of my friends and family."[3]

Celebrities Flaunt the Freeloader Mentality

Celebrities may not wind up in jail like politicians, but some have finessed the freeloader lifestyle to high art. "Some stars," writes Elisa Lipsky-Karasz in the *New York Post*, "eat, fly, sleep, party, do virtually everything in their day-to-day life for free."[4]

"It's at fever pitch right now," says Lori Majewski of *Us Weekly*. Many stars and would-be celebrities, she writes, "don't even understand that you 'buy' things anymore."[5]

At least one person has had it with the freeloading celebs. Britney Spears, reports Lipsky-Karasz, had a favorite coffee shop in New York's Greenwich Village. Spears frequented the caffeine house so often, she finally decided she shouldn't have to pay anymore.

"Don't you know who I am?" Spears reportedly asked the cashier one day.

"Yes," the person at the cash register replied, "but you still must pay. Sorry."[6]

We "Common" Folks Get In on the Act Too

Hosea could have been describing our own age when he wrote,

> "Like priests, like people"—since the priests are wicked, the people are wicked, too. So now I will punish both priests and people for all their wicked deeds. They will eat and still be hungry. Though they do a big business as prostitutes, they will have no children, for they have deserted the LORD to worship other gods. Alcohol and prostitution have robbed my people of their brains.
>
> Hosea 4:9–11 NLT

It's not just the politicians and celebrities infected by the freeloading spirit. They are the priests of secular society, so it should surprise no one that they set the trends others rush to embrace.

Take, for example, the lottery and gambling craze now addicting to many. The drain from this freeloading-inspired sickness is immense. The Mississippi Gulf Coast saw a 69 percent increase in domestic violence after the arrival of casinos. Professor John Warren Kindt told a congressional committee, "A business with 1,000 workers can anticipate increased personnel costs of $500,000 or more per year—simply by having various forms of legalized gambling activities accessible to its workers."[7]

Welfare fraud is another symptom of the freeloading spirit. In 1996, there was an attempt to reform America's welfare system. The need was urgent. Since the opening salvo in the war on poverty in the Johnson administration, the nation has spent $8.29 trillion on various welfare programs. But instead of defeating poverty, the programs spurred greater drain, providing opportunity for the freeloading mentality to divert vital resources from people genuinely in need of help.

And it's not just individuals playing the welfare game. Corporations have honed their freeloading spirit as well. "Corporate welfare" has become the tag for the practice. "Once companies are successful in securing a stream of taxpayer goodies, they defend their stake year after year with the help of their state's congressional delegation," noted the Cato Institute.[8]

How did the freeloading spirit so easily grip the heart of a nation once characterized by selflessness and heroic sacrifice? The freeloader attitude is the grabby child resulting from the sordid affair between consumerism and victimization.

The consumerist question is "What have you done for me lately?" The victimization attitude is "I am wronged by God, my parents, my spouse, my society, my teachers, my boss, etc., and therefore I deserve a free ride."

Marry those two and you have a brat—the freeloader.

Jesus and the Freeloaders

Jesus didn't come "to be served, but to serve, and to give His life a ransom for many" (Mark 10:45). And the freeloaders latched on wherever Jesus went.

Barbara Oakley says there is a type of the freeloader species known as the "hitchhiker." Freeloaders, she says,

> are relatively benign, can often be firmly guided to do reasonably good work, and can even become your friends. However, hitchhikers are completely different people—ones who can work their way into your confidence and then destroy it.[9]

Standing out there on the edge of the crowds around Jesus were people who dared to call him "Lord," or "Master." Their behavior indicated they hadn't bought totally into Jesus' teaching. "Why do you call Me, 'Lord, Lord,' and do not do what I say?" he asked them one day (Luke 6:46).

He knew some of them hung on because he was a miracle worker (see John 6:2). Others wanted to see if Jesus would ignite a revolution to overthrow the Romans. There were those who—like the Palm Sunday branch wavers—were on board as long as Jesus was popular.

Some of these people blocked those who were in real need. At Capernaum, friends had to rip the roof off a house to lower in a deathly ill man who couldn't get to Jesus because of the crushing crowd of freeloaders (see Mark 2:4).

Jesus always had his share of hitchhikers. Like a vagrant who flags down a car and tries to take advantage of the generous driver, Jesus' hitchhikers were there only to destroy him.

Jesus confronted the freeloaders in an effort to bring them into genuine discipleship. He gave them a parable to show how they could change. But to the hitchhikers, Jesus gave a firm "Hop off!" There will be those at the end of time whose exposed deeds prove they were not only along for the ride; they also actually opposed Jesus. He will say to them,

> "Depart from Me, accursed ones, into the eternal fire which has been prepared for the devil and his angels; for I was hungry, and you gave Me nothing to eat; I was thirsty, and you gave Me nothing to drink; I was a stranger, and you did not invite Me in; naked, and you did not clothe Me; sick, and in prison, and you did not visit Me." Then they themselves also will answer, "Lord, when did we see You hungry, or thirsty, or a stranger, or naked, or sick, or in prison, and did not take care of You?" Then He will answer them, "Truly I say to you, to the extent that you did not do it to one of the least of these, you did not do it to Me."
>
> Matthew 25:41–45

Jesus charged the freeloaders by giving them a compelling vision and challenging them to genuine discipleship. Jesus showed the hitchhikers the door.

It's Time for a Refill

When the freeloaders have almost stopped your forward motion.

Christopher Avery reports, "When well-performing people recognize a partner is a freeloader, they actually reduce their own commitment to that project's goals, and increase their attention and commitment to other areas of work."[10]

The reason, says Avery, is we want our efforts to be successful, and we know freeloaders drag things downward, hindering success. Therefore, we tend to move on to tasks at which we can succeed. This means trimming back our coattails if necessary, leaving the freeloaders behind.

So when your attention flags on projects that used to energize you to a full run, you know the freeloaders are draining you.

When the freeloaders keep hanging on.

There are coattail riders who refuse to be shaken off. Sometimes we call them "pests." You probably know the type. Just about the time you think you've left the freeloaders behind, you look back and find them clinging to your coattails. You can't shake them loose.

The freeloading drainers are getting to you when they just keep "hanging on," no matter how hard you try to shake them.

When you're the only one stocking the cupboard.

In congressional testimony, then-Federal Reserve chairman Alan Greenspan worried the "dramatic demographic change" coming to America "is certain to place enormous demands on our nation's resources."[11]

Greenspan's concern was that seventy-seven million baby boomers would begin drawing Social Security by 2012. The number of people paying into the program would be outnumbered by those taking benefits.[12]

You too may be struggling with the awareness that the people helping you stock the cupboard of your organization, group, or family are becoming takers more than contributors.

The warning light on your emotional energy tank is flashing when you feel like the freeloaders are subtracting faster than you can add.

Dealing with Freeloaders

Hit the Freeloaders with the Hard Facts

Barbara Oakley says that with freeloaders, including the hitchhiker variety, you must "set firm, explicit expectations, then stick to your guns."[13]

Jesus made it plain to his followers that he was ferreting

out the freeloaders when he said, "He who does not take his cross and follow after Me is not worthy of Me. . . . If anyone wishes to come after Me, he must deny himself, and take up his cross daily and follow Me" (Matt. 10:38).

Jesus held back nothing regarding his expectations, and neither should you as you confront the freeloaders. Once he told a crowd,

> If you want to be my follower you must love me more than your own father and mother, wife and children, brothers and sisters—yes, more than your own life. Otherwise, you cannot be my disciple. And you cannot be my disciple if you do not carry your own cross and follow me. But don't begin until you count the cost.
>
> Luke 14:26–28 NLT

As a thresher to a field of wheat, these words sift out the draining folk who cling to you like chaff.

Seek Commitment, Not Mere Compliance

Freeloaders will usually comply with your expectations as long as they can see a return in their future. But when the road gets bumpy, they're the first to hop off your bandwagon.

Commitment is the sharing of your passion, whereas compliance is merely submitting to your rules when it's in the interest of the freeloader to do so.

Jesus drew the line between commitment and compliance when he told his followers, "If they persecuted Me, they will also persecute you" (John 15:20). When danger looms, the committed person will die with you, but the freeloader will run from you.

Dare to Ask the Freeloaders for Sacrifice

Jesus didn't pull back from confronting freeloaders with the need to sacrifice. "Teacher, I will follow you no matter where you go," a scribe said to him one day. Jesus replied,

"Foxes have dens to live in, and birds have nests, but I, the Son of Man, have no home of my own, not even a place to lay my head" (Matt. 8:19–20 NLT).

I (Shaun) learned about sacrifice from Teresa. I will never forget the first time I saw her. I walked into a Florida church while the praise team was rehearsing and saw a beautiful woman in an Air Force flight suit. Then and there I determined to marry her.

As I got to know Teresa, I understood why she was a captain in the Air Force. Her father and two sisters also had military careers. Her whole family was characterized by a willingness to sacrifice for their country. Seeing her commitment renewed my attitude about the mission God had given me to minister to students.

Jesus said, "The last shall be first, and the first last" (Matt. 20:16). In his cause, the least are the greatest.

There's no room for freeloaders in an enterprise demanding sacrifice.

Cut Loose the Freeloaders Even If It Whittles Down Your Army

The Bible says some who heard Jesus and the hard facts about his mission turned away (see John 6:66). At times, Jesus seemed intentional in whittling down his group of followers.

Centuries before, Gideon had been challenged to do the same thing. Through him, God kept chipping away until the only army left was a small remnant who would do nothing but depend on him and fight by his power. Such troops won't run in the fury of battle.

I (Wallace) discovered this truth as I spent ten years traveling in twenty-one nations, helping train leaders. Most of the countries were on the frontiers of the gospel. I never felt worthy to be in the presence of the men and women I met.

There were people like Pastor Oomen, who had gone to the north of his nation of India as a missionary, leaving beautiful Kerala, the southern state where he was born. Radical Hindus beat Oomen and at one point stabbed him and left him for dead. But Oomen got up, tended his scars, and kept preaching. Ultimately he established a Bible college in the New Delhi region to train his countrymen to plant churches in their villages.

In Slovakia, my translator was a young woman who described being baptized in the Communist era. She took her stand for Christ at midnight in a river so cold the ice had to be knocked aside.

All over the world, such people are turning things upside down—just like their spiritual forebears.

And there's not a freeloader among them.

16

PATRONIZERS

Patronizers inflate your balloon primarily to pop it. The fatter the ego, the louder the bang. The bigger the gas bag, the larger the target.

As a child, I (Shaun) played sports. There were patronizers in my circle. I would fall, fumble the football, and come up with a mouthful of mud and grass, and the patronizers would applaud how quickly I untangled my feet as a form of mocking my skills as a ball carrier.

"He couldn't catch a ball if he had hands the size of skillets, but he can sure hop up fast when he falls. After all, he's had plenty of practice," they seemed to say.

Had I mistaken their arrogance for adulation, I would have been fooled into thinking they considered me a hero.

My father was no patronizer. "Son, you caught four passes today, and I am mighty proud of you," he might say. "But why did you drop the fifth throw?"

The patronizers taught me nothing, but I grew through my dad's honesty.

Patronizers, Flatterers, and Sycophants

Patronizers, flatterers, and sycophants run in the same pack.

William Hazlitt was an eighteenth-century political radical and essayist, but he saw through the patronizers, flatterers, and sycophants. He called them "counterfeits in friendship."[1]

Patronizers consider themselves superior to you, so don't confuse patronizers as patrons. The latter support you, but patronizers feign encouragement through a wicked, subtle style called condescension.

Flatterers aren't really focused on you; they merely want to lavish you with praise to promote their own interests.

Sycophants are yes-people either because they are too afraid to say no—since they are currying favor to manipulate you—or because they are generally servile. They will just as soon say yes to Hitler as to you.

Hazlitt spotlighted the characteristics of this seductive family of drainers as follows:

- They watch for your flaws, but rather than showing you a better way, they use them to betray you. It's easy to assume the people who pump you with praise believe you can walk on water, but they are on a constant search for the holes in your hull not to repair them but to enlarge the leaky spots.
- They are "treacherous and fickle." You think the grinding and hammering you hear is their labor to build you up, while it's really the undercutting of your foundations.

- They go from devotion to distaste. They may begin in your cheering section, but eventually they gravitate to the opposing team.[2]

Despite the drain, undiscerning leaders fill their courts with the patronizing, flattering yes-people.

England's fourteenth-century King Richard II was drained by the bad counsel coming from the "treacherous and fickle" folk around him. He offended the nobility with his grabs for power, and eventually some of them brought legal action against him to try to have him deposed. The monarch's supporters couldn't deny some of his foolish actions, but they argued that the problem lay with the sycophants surrounding him. Shakespeare, as one of Richard's defenders, said, "The king is not himself, but basely led by flatterers."[3]

The king had created a climate in which the patronizing, flattering, sycophantic family grew like mold in a hothouse. A letter writer in *Business Week* described that atmosphere as one created by leaders who have "a false sense of self-importance, arrogance, entitlement, and the ability to influence their personal economic gain."[4]

Such leaders' delusional view of themselves includes the notion they are messianic. The salvation of the world—or at least their organizational slice of it—is on their shoulders. It's no surprise author and researcher Jim Collins found that CEOs with such a warped understanding of themselves are not the most effective leaders.[5] They attract the patronizers, flatterers, and sycophants, and ultimately the leaders and their companies are drained.

Arrogance at the top feeds the patronizing, flattering, sycophantic culture. Such an attitude will demand the servile spirit that encourages the sycophants especially. Throughout his ministry, Jesus stressed the importance of a teachable attitude, not an arrogant one. A major qualification for elders, or leaders, in the developing church was that they be teachable. The people who "get it" regarding the kingdom of God must be childlike (see Mark 10:15).

When those in charge have a sense of entitlement, they are as pompous as a royal family. Those around them are afraid to tell the emperor he is naked. The entitlement-conscious leaders want the flatterers, believing the adoration is due them.

Also, leaders who manipulate the system for their own gain are a set-up for patronizers, flatterers, and sycophants. Manuel Velasquez, a professor of business ethics, traced the Enron collapse at least partly to the "boom culture" of the 1990s:

> During periods like these, our moral standards tend to get corrupted. The ease with which we see money being made leads us to cut corners, to take shortcuts, to become focused on getting our own share of the pie no matter what because everybody else is getting theirs. This general boom culture, I believe, was part of what affected Enron and led its managers and executives to think that anything was okay so long as the money kept rolling in.[6]

Enron's top executives implied that employees at lower levels committed the actions that wiped out the company. Whatever the case, the climate attracted drainers who deluded themselves as they lined their pockets.

Jesus and the Patronizers

Condescension is a form of arrogance toward one considered inferior, and it greeted Jesus everywhere he went. For example, when he traveled to Jerusalem for the Feast of Tabernacles, there were those who rejected his messiahship on the grounds "we know where this man is from" (John 7:27). As we noted earlier, they only thought they knew. Their notion was he came from Galilee rather than the prophesied Bethlehem—Jesus' true birthplace.

When Nicodemus challenged his fellow religious leaders to be open to Jesus, they smirked, "No prophet arises out of Galilee" (v. 52).

Then there was Nathanael, whose first response upon hearing of Jesus was "Can any good thing come out of Nazareth?" (John 1:46). The good news is Nathanael—a man without hidden agendas (see v. 47)—went from patronizing to committed discipleship when he "checked out" Jesus at Philip's urging.

People will be condescending and patronizing toward you when they think where you're from automatically disqualifies you from leading them.

The Patronizing Flatterers

On one of their many forays to trick Jesus, the Pharisees tried flattery. "Teacher, we know that You are truthful and teach the way of God in truth, and defer to no one; for You are not partial to any" (Matt. 22:16). Then they posed the question they had hoped would snare Jesus: "Tell us then, what do You think? Is it lawful to give a poll-tax to Caesar, or not?" (v. 17).

Few flattering scams are as effective as the title gambit. Flatterers may call you "Your Majesty" to schmooze you. When Jesus heard his enemies call him "Teacher," he knew something other than honoring him was on their agenda. They were simply patronizing Jesus to set him up for what they were sure would be humiliation. But Jesus saw through their plot, and one more time they were foiled.

George Washington, America's revolutionary leader and first president, had to fight the temptation to yield to the titling mania of the flatterers. One writer declared him "the American Zeus, Moses and Cincinnatus all rolled into one."[7] Vice President John Adams said Washington should be called "His Highness, the President of the United States and Protector of their Liberties." But Washington preferred simply "Mr. President."[8]

Resist the layering on of titles. They only give the patronizers more targets to shoot down.

The Patronizing Sycophants

Jesus wearied of the sycophants. At one point he said to some of them, "Why do you call Me, 'Lord, Lord,' and do not do what I say?" (Luke 6:46). Here he uncovered the core of the sycophantic spirit: yes-people are primarily about words, not actions. They will tell you yes to win your favor but then do as they please.

Jesus challenged the sycophants to put their money where their mouth was.

It's Time for a Refill

When you start falling for the lines the flatterers throw at you.

"My voice coach tells me I can go all the way, that I am the next American Idol," a young woman told the panel of judges on the popular TV show. "My friends also say I'm great," she added. Then she opened her mouth to sing.

Teresa and I (Shaun) were dumbfounded. "Why would her coach and friends tell her she had a great voice and let her be humiliated on national television?" I asked Teresa.

"No one wanted to hurt her feelings," my wife replied.

That was only part of the problem. The real issue is the young woman fell for the delusion sold her by her money-making coach and flattering, sycophantic friends.

You're almost drained when you listen to the voices of the flatterers rather than your own screech.

When you make compromises to keep the sycophant saying yes.

The fall of Rome has been analyzed since the first thud of cracking granite. One of the factors was that of an increasingly deviant, degenerate, drained chief executive.

Moral exhaustion resulted from the pressure on the emperors to allow their sycophantic cronies and citizens to have their excesses. Jim Nelson Black writes the Roman rulers believed potentially revolutionary people "had to be fed and amused to prevent violent outbursts." They "resorted to the form of bribery known as bread and circuses in order to keep the masses under control."[9] In the end, the desperation of the rulers to keep the sycophants happy drained Rome of financial resources and moral capital.

Leadership expert Warren Bennis says 70 percent of followers won't question their leader even when they can see he's about to err.[10] The impact on leaders of such a sycophantic following is the drive to hold on to their "admirers" no matter the cost.

When you are willing to do almost anything—including compromise cherished principles—to keep people happy, they will tap heavily into your emotional vitality.

When you mistake the patronizers' put-downs as compliments.

Remember, patrons may be genuine supporters, but patronizers are condescending. They talk down to you.

"I liked your opera," Mozart said to the composer after listening to it. Just as the man puffed with pride, Mozart finished his thought. "Perhaps I will set it to music."

An actress told Ilka Chase, regarding her most recent book, "I enjoyed it immensely. Who wrote it for you?"

"I'm glad you liked it," Chase replied. "Who read it to you?"[11]

The patronizers have seriously sapped your discerning prowess as well as your emotional energy when you fall into the delusion of believing a put-down is a compliment.

Dealing with Flatterers

Be Discerning: Know the Type

Many a group has been wiped out by a leader who couldn't sort out the varieties of people around him or her. Responses must always be appropriate. You must know with whom you're dealing. You may choose a rapier to thrust back at the patronizer, but a sword jab is not what the sycophant needs—especially if he or she is a frightened person who says yes only because of the fear of saying no.

A lady we'll call Lynn grew up as this type of person. Her father was a domineering, arrogant, brutal man who strutted like a rooster. She trembled in his presence. When Lynn grew up, she married a man just like her dad. Now she had two men to fear. Then she got a job where her boss was cut from the same cloth as her father and spouse. Lynn labored to please all three.

One day her boss—call him Mr. Meany—summoned Lynn. "Get me five thousand copies of this contract run off by six p.m.," he ordered.

Though she had only an hour and a half to complete the task, she sighed and said, "Yes, sir."

"How dare you patronize me like that!" said Mr. Meany. Actually, Lynn was responding from her fear, not from condescension. In fact, Lynn was far too frightened to be condescending. Mr. Meany failed to recognize the type of person he was addressing and devastated the knock-kneed woman.

To turn the drain of the patronizers, flatterers, and sycophants to gain, be smarter than Mr. Meany. Know your people and engage with them appropriately. Don't lump them all in the same pile. Servile sycophants especially are recoverable.

Judas Iscariot may have seen a groveling sycophant when Mary Magdalene poured costly perfume over Jesus' feet and bathed them with her hair, but Jesus saw a woman with great potential. He discerned the nature of her motives and actions. Rather than castigating Mary, the Lord complimented her.

Don't Let the Patronizers Frame the Issue

Every patronizer Jesus faced was trying to get the jump on him. They wanted to frame the Sabbath issue, the tax policy, or the matter of authority. But Jesus refused to let the put-down be the topic; instead he let it glance off him and went on to the topic he selected.

The Pharisees wanted to hit Jesus with the question of paying taxes to Caesar. Jesus knew the real issue was their hypocrisy. He skimmed over the tax-paying controversy with a brilliant sentence, but he put a searing spotlight on his questioners' double-mindedness.

Framing the issue means you, not someone else, determine the topic. Years ago, I (Wallace) encountered this struggle. I had the uncomfortable task of trying to coordinate a meeting of the president's domestic Cabinet officers in Atlanta. It was important the session be confidential since it involved people who were meeting with the Cabinet officers at some risk.

The press crowded the hotel where the attorney general of the United States and his colleagues were assembled. At one point I had to stand at the door of the conference room and stand off the reporters. As I tried to explain the nature of the meeting and the need for confidentiality, a reporter tried to frame a new issue. Sticking a microphone in my face, he asked, "Is this the way you practice censorship?"

Censorship, of course, was not the issue. The issue was the need to resolve a sensitive, difficult problem in a vigorous debate that could be possible only without the cameras.

Good leaders refuse to be drawn aside. Whether it's flattery, rudeness, or groveling, they stay on subject.

"Know Thyself"

The flatterers tried to tease Jesus with his growing influence over the people. He could lead the overthrow of Rome and win himself an earthly kingdom. But Jesus refused the seductions of the flatterers because he knew who he was and from where he had come. As he stood before Pilate, he told the Roman procurator, "My kingdom is not of this world. If My kingdom were of this world, then My servants would be fighting so that I would not be handed over to the Jews; but as it is, My kingdom is not of this realm" (John 18:36).

"So you are a king?" Pilate asked Jesus.

"You say that I am a king, and you are right," Jesus responded (v. 37 NLT). But Jesus refused to allow Pilate to determine the kind of king he was. Jesus knew he was the king of truth and told Pilate so.

Knowing the truth about yourself keeps you from floating down the drain on the lavishing swirls the flatterers spin around you.

Challenge the Sycophants to Action

The best way to stop the siphoning of the sycophants is to demand actions rather than words. Someday every tongue will confess Jesus as Lord, but ultimately he challenges people to prove their acclamations by their deeds.

Sometimes sycophants are stymied by their love of dispensing accolades, which they believe to be their purpose and contribution. To allow them to get away with that assumption is enabling behavior. It blocks the sycophant from understanding his or her own potential.

Responsible leaders find ways to get people beyond their affirming words to responsible actions. The key phrase here is "responsible leaders." Leaders who fall for the scam and are drained by the patronizers, flatterers, and sycophants have no one to blame but themselves.

17

POT STIRRERS

"Terry Tempest" was a young man in a student ministry I (Shaun) led. When mistruths spread like a forest fire, I almost always found the smoldering match in Terry's hand. If there was an outbreak of conflict and division, I could count on Terry egging on both sides. Shock and sensationalism might send tremors through our organization, and Terry was sure to be doing the shaking.

"I hate Mexico," he muttered on a mission trip to that country, repeating the mantra until many of his fellow team members had taken up his glum outlook. "The food is horrible, and it'll make you really sick" was the rumor, and there was Terry at its headwaters.

I concluded the young man wasn't happy unless he was stirring the pot. There are many like that. Business psychologist Paul Kenneth Glass says such people have a "constant need to stir up others. [They] are seldom comfortable unless there is some form of chaos to capitalize on, if only to make someone else look bad."[1]

The Pot-Stirring Problem

There are four ways pot stirrers drain you.

Rumor Mongering

Pot stirrers spin the panic that makes rumors boil over. The unknown is a big point the stirrers can exploit. "The critical variables in a successful organizational design are control and guidance in the face of uncertainty," write Noel M. Tichy and Mary Anne Devanna. "Organizations must be designed either to reduce uncertainty or to absorb it."[2]

Tichy and Devanna list three types of uncertainties that can set the rumor pot seething. *Technical uncertainty* affects efficiency and effectiveness. *Political uncertainty* goes to the core of authority and control of your group. *Cultural uncertainty* impacts the belief system and values that drive the organization.

Effective leaders identify the areas of uncertainty and do all possible to remove or reduce the unknown quantities. This, in turn, removes the pots from the organizational stove, reducing the number of those the stirrers can set twirling.

Leaders do this by

1. eliminating plans and tasks beyond the group's competency and strength;
2. establishing clearly understood procedures;
3. putting in place a well-defined decision process and stable governance;
4. making sure everyone in the organization aligns with its beliefs and values.

Actions like these take away indefinites, leading to a proportionate reduction in the potential for rumor mongering.

Pot stirrers often grumble over a piece of the puzzle they can't see fitting anywhere, so give them the whole picture.

Lie Festering

This version of the pot stirrer is like a puppy I (Wallace) once observed. The owner adopted the pup, which was just getting over a case of mange, from a rescue agency. The new master worked hard to cure the little animal and finally got the skin disorder down to a few small irritations. However, finishing the healing process was almost impossible because the dog kept scratching at the small sores until they reopened and the pain intensified.

Similarly, some pot stirrers keep lies bleeding and festering until the whole organization is infected.

Strife Sowing

Sixty-five percent of work-performance problems and as much as 42 percent of employee time is spent resolving conflict, according to the Dana Mediation Institute.[3]

The average workplace is a big pot full of spicy ingredients ready to stir. Mitch is at the precipice of divorce and arrives at work after a night battling his wife. Debbie's fiancé lost his job. Sheree's mother is dying. Jackson's investments have cratered. People often bring such personal problems into an already boiling workplace, therefore stoking the strife.

Pot stirrers roam the halls, searching for situations to exploit. They're like an anti-Johnny Appleseed. The character from American folklore scattered delicious seed wherever he went, leaving whole orchards in his wake. But pot stirrers leave a tempest behind and smirk with satisfaction as they watch the sparks fly.

Sensationalism Igniting

Physician Charles E. Reed shocked a committee of the U.S. House of Representatives when he told them, "Some surgeons, anesthesiologists, nurses and other health professionals have become terrified of their workplace." The reason, said Dr. Reed, was "the sensationalism that has developed around latex allergy." Sensationalists had promoted the notion that "exposure to rubber in any form might kill them."[4]

Dr. Reed said he had examined patients complaining of "latex allergy," yet they had no allergens present in their body—even under heavy exposure to latex. "For these unfortunate people, the fear generated by the sensationalism is more disabling than the disease would ever be," he told the members of Congress.[5]

Sensationalists aren't limited to the medical profession. They're in all organizations and will seize on a ripple to create a tidal wave.

Jesus and the Pot Stirrers

Rumor Mongers

First-century Jerusalem was a bubbling pot. Light an ember of gossip in its bustling market lanes, and the tale leaped from tongue to tongue like flame hopping over pieces of dry kindling. No wonder James wrote, "The tongue is a fire, the very world of iniquity; the tongue is set among our members as that which defiles the entire body, and sets on fire the course of our life, and is set on fire by hell" (James 3:6).

Pot stirrers who use rumor can set a whole organization ablaze with distortions, leading to dead-end strategies and wasting of resources to meet challenges that do not exist.

Jesus was thinking of the rumor mongers as he and his disciples walked one day along the slopes of the Mount of Olives. A short distance to the west, across the Kidron Valley, they could see the temple complex astride Mount Moriah like a great treasure chest. Jesus talked to his team about the future and the rumors they would face (see Matt. 24:4–8).

There would be many pretenders to the messiahship, Jesus warned, all coming with the claim, "I am the Christ." Further, there would be unsettling rumors of war and strife, of tribulation and sorrow. "See to it that no one misleads you," he said (v. 4).

To be misled by rumor is to have one's thoughts twisted, to allow reality's foundations to be chipped away, and to have truth painted over with so many coats of lies it disappears altogether.

But Jesus said his followers were to remain steady, not running after all the speculations that would cause the very air to sizzle. They would overcome rumors by "seeing." The New Testament Greek word for *see* means discerning, perceiving, discovering, and understanding what is going on around you.[6]

Jesus' people won't be burned by the cinders of rumor if they stop and think. Rather than chasing after rumor, they are to investigate its claims and wait until they understand what is going on. If the followers of Christ do that, they won't be drained by the pot-stirring rumor mongers.

Lie Festerers

Jesus showed it's vital to confront lie festerers quickly and head-on.

John reported on a conversation Jesus had with "those Jews who had believed Him" (John 8:31). As the conversation developed, he told them, "You are of your father the devil, and you want to do the desires of your father. . . . He is a liar and the father of lies" (v. 44).

Why would Jesus call people who "had believed Him" sons and daughters of the master deceiver? The clue is in Jesus' statement, "If God were your Father, you would love Me" (v. 42). They had "believed" Jesus, but they did not love him. Therefore, the group Jesus addressed was led astray by lies and then festered them.

Among the greatest drainers you will face are those who believe you but do not value you. What you say to them makes no difference. Because they don't care for you and your values, they will eagerly promote deceit to deflate your cause. In fact, they may consider it in their interest to do so.

Strife Sowers

Paul opened his letter to the Corinthian church by telling the people he had to address them as "infants in Christ" (1 Cor. 3:1). "Jealousy and strife" marked them as immature (v. 3).

Anyone who has watched small children at play would understand. They begin innocently but then get bored with togetherness. They start picking and jabbing at one another, calling each other names, and pitting groups against one another until the parent, teacher, or other responsible person has to quell the riot.

One day Jesus' disciples revealed the "infants" they were by arguing over who was on top. "There was also a strife among them, which of them should be accounted the greatest" (Luke 22:24). Jesus shut them down in a hurry. The greatest, he told them, is not the one at the top, but the person at the bottom—the servant of all.

Jesus showed that wise leaders recognize what drives pot stirrers to stoke strife. It may be their own sense of inadequacy. Being able to control other people to the point they can be pitted against one another makes the strife sower feel strong.

By pointing out who is really great, Jesus showed his disciples what mature people look like. Strife sowers need to be encouraged to grow up.

Sensationalism Igniters

"Lord, even the demons obey us when we use your name!" excited missionaries told Jesus upon return from their forays (Luke 10:17 NLT).

But Jesus told them they only thought they saw the spectacular. "'Yes,' he told them, 'I saw Satan falling from heaven as a flash of lightning!'" (v. 18 NLT). Perhaps he was revealing to them that he had seen the pre-creation plunge of Lucifer.

Jesus told the sensation igniters they needed to get things in perspective. "Don't rejoice just because evil spirits obey you; rejoice because your names are registered as citizens of heaven" (v. 20 NLT).

The drain exerted by sensation-igniting pot stirrers is the pull away from what is really important. The focus on the spectacular takes passion away from the mundane daily grind, where battles are really won and goals are genuinely accomplished.

Sensationalists want to stay up on the Mount of Transfiguration, watching the wonder of the glorious Son of God surrounded by the heroes of heaven (see Matt. 17:1–9). But the Jesus who takes us up the mountain also brings us down to the valley, where discipleship is lived out.

It's Time for a Refill

When you simmer most of the time.

I (Wallace) began my professional career in the newspaper business. I became an editorial writer for a large daily newspaper. I pondered with my peers the events and people making the news, and I wrote my opinions. Then I moved to the "other side" of the desk, working in government for the newsmakers I had once covered and opined about.

Decades of thinking about current events focused me intently on public affairs and the state of the nation, about which I fretted a great deal. At one point I found myself stewing so much I had to turn off the talk shows and find a means of being informed that allowed me to turn down the heat.

I was being drained by my constant indignation. I discovered I not only hated the political foes' ideas but also disdained the people themselves. That was not a Christlike attitude, and I had to stop simmering.

Certainly we should be socially aware and involved in public affairs—even in politics—but the pot stirrers mustn't be permitted to control the heat. What simmers too long becomes nothing but vapor, and no substance is left.

When you feel you're managing a rumor mill.

"Terry Tempest," the rumor mongerer I (Shaun) introduced to you earlier, wanted to go on our annual ski trip. Not wanting to exclude anyone, I reluctantly agreed, with some conditions.

"I can't let you be a negative influence on this trip," I told Terry in a meeting with him and his parents. I then told his parents, "It's an eight-hour drive to the ski area, but if Terry creates even the slightest problem, you must drive up and get him." All agreed.

Within hours of our arrival at the resort, Terry was stirring pots everywhere. I was exhausted as I sought to still the turmoil. Sadly, the only way to turn off the machinery cranking out the distortions was to phone Terry's parents, who drove up and took the pot stirrer home.

When you spend more time as a referee than a leader.

The strife-sowing pot stirrers lure you into the ring, where you become the fight referee who gets a bloody nose. I (Wallace) discovered this in the first church I served as a pastor. It was among the most promising in the state and needed a master plan for growth of the facilities.

Soon factions developed. One group wanted to limit expansion and pour money into a small, elegant structure.

Another wanted to build a barnlike, austere structure that would accommodate huge numbers.

Within a year, I was no longer a visionary pastor but a referee holding off warring groups. I jumped into the ring and got so bloodied I hopped back out, wondering if I had the strength to try to lead another church.

When sensationalism sets your agenda.

The lure of the sensational is among the most dangerous pot-stirring gimmicks because it's so subtle.

History shows how churches and other organizations get drained by sensationalism. In the late second century AD, a man named Montanus emerged in Asia Minor, ultimately claiming to be the voice of the Holy Spirit. Montanus would "prophesy" while in a trance, and he began to attract followers like Prisca and Maximilla, who left their husbands to follow the new "prophet." Among the draining results of Montanus and his claims was the discrediting of genuine prophecy and apocalyptic literature, including the book of Revelation.

Sensationalists not only erode trust and confidence; they siphon energy through the expectations they create. In a church, for example, sensationalism will stir curiosity to see how the ecstasies of last week can be topped this week.

Leaders who allow sensationalists to set their agendas are drained in trying to pull increasingly larger rabbits from their hats.

Dealing with Pot Stirrers

Turn Off the Flame under the Pot

Be proactive rather than reactive by creating an environment where everyone knows everything possible and the rumors have no basis.

Jesus said, "You will know the truth, and the truth will make you free" (John 8:32). Truth will always snuff out rumors and lies.

"Unwarranted rumors can be real killers of productivity and morale," write Rod Walsh and Dan Carrison. Yet many leaders are silent as a rock while "whispering campaigns spread through their organizations like a cancer."[7]

Some leaders don't talk because they believe it's "beneath their dignity to comment on company gossip."[8] Others think their response would only give credence to the rumors. Sometimes the rumors and distortions become so unsettling to the whole organization that the leader at last must speak up. But he or she seems merely to be staving off collapse. "We must really be in trouble if the boss is responding to the rumors," some employees may say. More rumor mongering is the result.

Organizations have these problems because they do not have a communications environment, which consists of the following steps:

1. A senior leader meets regularly with his or her core team—managers, supervisors, and team leaders—for the sake of keeping them informed about what is happening in the organization.
2. The management team convenes its subordinates on a regular basis to share the information.
3. Publications present the facts in easy-to-understand formats so organizational members can read and digest as well as hear the information.
4. Leaders often convene one-on-one or small group gatherings to get feedback on members' understanding of what they're hearing.

A strong flow of information puts out the fires and settles the pots.

Focus on the Facts, Not the Pot Stirrer

Anxiety is a huge flame under the rumor pot. The pot stirrers will try to turn up the heat, but facts overcome anxiety. Walsh and Carrison write,

> The best way to stop rumors is to prevent anxiety from taking hold in the first place—and that can only be accomplished by a manager who has never lied to his or her people. Managers who build a reputation of credibility—and who share with their employees both the good news and, perhaps even more important, the bad news—are an organization's best bet against the loss of productivity and valued personnel due to unfounded rumors.[9]

Leaders who try to spin the focus away from the facts by talking only about the misbehavior of the pot stirrer lose their credibility. Followers who know that their leadership will always give them the full portrait—"warts and all"—have a high level of trust.

Don't Let the Pot Stirrer Become Your Confidant

A fellow I'll (Wallace) call Chad joined a church I served as pastor. He said he shared our vision and wanted to be part of an innovative, exciting church.

He flattered, yessed, and patronized himself into my confidence. I thought we would storm the gates of hell arm in arm. Foolishly I let him know my future dreams, my discouragements over problems and failures, and my opinion on leaders who wouldn't get on the team.

Too late I learned Chad was a pot stirrer. He sought self-importance, and he used our conversations to make himself appear to be an "insider." I had to work hard to assure members of my staff that I had not disclosed to Chad plans they didn't know about. My failure to recognize this pot stirrer threatened the morale of other leaders in our church.

Eventually I had to distance myself from Chad. It was hurtful and draining. That's why Paul Kenneth Glass says never to take the pot stirrers into your confidence, "especially regarding your own personal or private concerns, [because they] will eventually be used against you."[10]

Pot stirring may seem mischievous fun, but it doesn't take long for it to turn into a huge drain. Put on the lid as quickly as you can.

18

QUITTERS

Quitters drain you by leaving, even after you've invested them with the best of your resources.

My (Shaun) son, Austin, is intensely competitive. Awhile back, he played water polo but wasn't the best swimmer and wanted to quit the team. Actually, he did quite well for a seven-year-old on a team of older boys. When I tried to encourage him, he replied, "But Dad, if I know I'm going to lose, I'd rather not play!"

"Austin, I'm glad you're so competitive," I said. "But you're not going to win every time. If you hate so much to lose, why don't you quit every sport? In fact, if you take that attitude, you'll want to quit life, because you'll discover you can't win every game and every battle."

I could see an intense expression on his face as he tried to absorb what I was telling him. "God is happy when you use the talents and gifts he's given you to the best of your ability, whether you win or not," I added.

As we'll see in a moment, there are many reasons people want to quit. But by focusing on God's significance rather than our own, our perspective shifts. We find ourselves persisting where once we would have pulled out.

The Quitter Phenomenon

The quitter phenomenon in our highly transitory culture has produced a crisis of undependability. Where once there was an ethos of grim determination to keep going no matter what, people find it easier to walk away from commitments too hard or distasteful. This presents a huge problem for leaders needing to count on people to follow through.

Management consultant Gregory P. Smith cites ten causes of the quitting phenomenon in the American workplace, ranging from managers piling on too much work to excluding workers from decision making. "Employees don't quit their companies," he says. "They quit their bosses."[1] But such explanations report more on symptoms of the quitting phenomenon than the real causes. In fact, there are seven major reasons people become quitters.

Burnout

Sir Walter Scott was speaking for hosts of people everywhere when he said, "I often wish that I could lie down and sleep without waking."[2] The eighteenth-century writer was fifty-six years old, his health was fading, and he was watching his wife die of an unstoppable illness. Scott's fortune had been wiped out in the collapse of a publishing venture. He asked his creditors for time and worked feverishly to write and publish, dedicating his royalties to pay off the debt.

Then his wife died. Never had the temptation to give up been so great. Scott, however, had made up his mind to die without debt rather than pass on the burden to his family.

"Were an enemy coming upon my house, would I not do my best to fight, although oppressed in spirits; and shall a similar despondency prevent me from mental exertion? It shall not, by heaven!"[3]

So despite the burnout, Scott pushed on. He died September 21, 1832, believing the debt was settled. Actually, it wasn't paid fully until 1847, with the sale of his copyrights.[4]

Not all will be as persistent as Sir Walter Scott. Burnout causes many to shut down. Wise leaders care enough about their team members to understand when burnout threatens and to take actions to lower the heat.

Change

Change "inevitably triggers an approach/avoidance tension," writes organizational leadership expert Noel M. Tichy.[5] That is, there will be some people within a group or team who will accept the need to change and others who will be threatened by it. Tension increases as the accepters want to move forward and the avoiders want to hold the line. Individuals must "unlearn and relearn, exchange power and status, and exchange old norms and values for new norms and values."[6] For some wanting to avoid change, the stretch is too much, and they become quitters.

At thirty-five, Pastor Randy unwittingly ignited approach/avoidance tension in his new church. He was ready to lead the church into dynamic growth, and with anticipation he accepted the call of First Community Church. Its position—in the heart of a small town growing rapidly as a bedroom community for a nearby metropolis—signaled a great future.

But not everyone in the congregation agreed. Old-timers fretted over the young families moving into their community. Still, Randy convinced a small majority—consisting mainly of the new people—to buy an expensive parcel of land along the highway leading to the metropolis for a large, new church complex.

Changes in worship style and programming had already become irritants to folks sacrificing old ways. When the vote came on the master plan, almost half the congregation voted with their feet—they walked out. Many of them had been longtime major contributors, so Randy and the congregation remaining were left with a huge debt. The approach/avoidance conflict sunk Pastor Randy's dreams.

Fear

Fear compels some people to give up and turn back from challenges and opportunities.

I (Wallace) watched Sarah Jane turn away from everything her heart desired, all because of fear. Her husband, Stan, walked out on her thirteen years into their marriage. Their children were just nudging adolescence, and she hunkered down to raise two boys as a single mom.

Eight years later, Sarah Jane met Robbie at church. His wife had died two years earlier, and he was ready for a new relationship. I saw them as they began sitting together in church, both aglow with the budding romance.

Within a few months, Robbie asked Sarah Jane to marry him. He loved her sons also and was willing to be a father to them. I knew Robbie to be a godly man who would provide well for Sarah Jane and her family.

But she turned down Robbie's proposal. She couldn't get past the fear of abandonment still gnawing at her over Stan's behavior. Fear drained Sarah Jane of hope, confidence, and a future. She and Robbie still sit together in church, and my prayer is that someday love will douse her fear. After all, the Scripture says, "Perfect love casts out fear" (1 John 4:18). Fear-soaked quitters need "perfect love," which encompasses two facets:

1. **Perfect love is complete love.** The New Testament Greek term for *perfect* signifies completeness in purpose. Perfect love embraces a person's totality—the body, mind, will, emotions, and spirit. Individuals who are loved this extensively aren't fearful, because they understand everything in them is known and treasured by the lover.
2. **Perfect love is unconditional love.** The Holy Spirit inspired John to pen the highest Greek word for "love," *agape*, which refers to love without conditions. An individual who knows there is no small print in a relationship becomes secure, and fear fades.

Disagreement with the Strategic Elements

People will quit when there is radical disagreement with your vision, mission, goals, and strategies, or any combination thereof.

Effective leaders try to understand why people disagree. Often it's because of the personalities involved. Author Edgar H. Schein notes three orientations of human personality that may spark disagreement, leading to nonalignment with your group's strategic elements.

1. **The Doing Orientation.** These are the "can do" folk who believe leaders ought to take charge and be in firm control. They are frustrated and tempted to quit when they believe leadership is waffling or lacks confidence.
2. **The Being Orientation.** These people are the existentialists who are focused on a here and now that cannot be changed and that human beings must accept. When leaders try to transform organizations and circumstances, these folk may walk out with a shrug, believing change to be impossible.

3. **The Being-in-Becoming Orientation.** These are the individuals who seek to align with their environment through the development of personal abilities. They may be the least likely to quit but will leave if they conclude they are a "misfit." They are most likely to have a spiritual orientation.[7]

Discomfort with Style

John Mark was one of the Bible's noted quitters. He had accompanied Paul and Barnabas on their first missionary journey. But when they launched out on a mission to minister primarily to Gentiles, John Mark pulled out, perhaps because he disagreed with the cultural shift of taking the gospel to non-Jews.

Later, when Paul and Barnabas were heading out again, Barnabas wanted to take John Mark, but Paul would have none of it. "Paul kept insisting that they should not take him along who had deserted them in Pamphylia and had not gone with them to the work" (Acts 15:38). Ultimately the powerful partnership of Paul and Barnabas split over the man Paul considered a quitter.

The discomforting style prompting people to quit may be the organization's culture. Jack Fitzenz, a human resource professional focusing on how to keep good employees, says, "The two reasons why most people leave a company are the supervisor and the culture."[8]

Craig, a laid-back man who enjoyed composing music, strumming his guitar, and hanging out with his leaders, discovered soon after he began his church job that he was in the wrong culture.

Craig became a staff member in the singles division of a megachurch. Within weeks, he was ready to quit. With more than five hundred people on staff, there was no opportunity for folksy interaction with church leadership. The constant calendaring of programming and plans flew in the face of his "just let it happen" style. Craig's supervisor wasn't surprised when he turned in his resignation and moved to a smaller congregation.

Craig was not a bad person or a deficient employee. His personality simply didn't align with the megachurch culture. Wisely, he chose to move on to a place more suited to his personal style.

Craig and people like him may have a being-in-becoming personality orientation. When they conclude they are misfits in a particular culture, they quit. However, such folk may not be quitters in a negative sense; rather, they are individuals who simply want to be in a setting that will maximize personal gifts and abilities.

Managerial style may also be a cause of discomfort. All ten of the reasons for quitting cited by Gregory P. Smith center on leadership. In fact, after listing his ten causes for people to quit their jobs, Smith says it's interesting that "all ten factors begin with the phrase, 'Management.'"[9]

Whether it's the boss or the culture, people out of sync with their environment are likely to move on.

Distraction

General George Washington faced immense hurdles when trying to build an army to face powerful British forces. One of the most perplexing challenges he faced was maintaining troop strength. His biggest foe was distraction.

Washington drew his soldiers from an agrarian economy. When times for planting and harvest rolled around, the fighters' hearts and minds turned homeward. They wondered who would sow the seed and reap the fruit that enabled their families to survive. In such seasons, Washington and his generals faced a huge drain on the army's strength as troops whose attention was pulled from the battlefield to the harvest field laid down their weapons and walked home.[10]

Failure

You won't find Harry Hartman in the baseball Hall of Fame, but he's in the game's history books. As a player for the Brooklyn Dodgers, Hartman had the shortest major league career in history.

One day in 1918, Hartman, who was playing for a minor league team, was summoned to pitch for the Dodgers against the Pittsburgh Pirates. The batter slapped Hartman's first major league pitch for a single. The next Pirate pounded a triple off Hartman, who then walked the next hitter. The following batter knocked a single.

The crowd watched as Hartman abandoned the game and walked from the pitcher's mound straight to the showers. From there, his arm still aching from pitches, Hartman walked to a naval recruiting station.

For Hartman, failure in his one moment on the pitcher's mound had made any thought of trying to continue in baseball impossible.[11]

Jesus and the Quitters

Quitters turned away from Jesus for various reasons.

Burnout

Jesus had a keen knowledge of human limitations. He understood the intensity of his assignment, its tasks, and what it could do to frail people.

One day the exhausted disciples reported back to Jesus after casting out demons, healing sick people, and serving others to the extent they didn't even have time to eat. Jesus looked at his tired followers and said, "Come away by yourselves to a secluded place and rest a while" (Mark 6:31).

When they arrived at the "secluded place," there was a crowd of five thousand hungry people. After feeding the multitude, Jesus once again looked at his men near burn-out. He told them to get on a boat and sail away, across the lake of Galilee.

Author Rich Lamb says, "Jesus wanted his disciples to learn that rest and ministry aren't incompatible."[12] Jesus demonstrated that wise leaders prevent people quitting due to burnout by "assigning" withdrawal and rest.

Changes He Brought

Some began following Jesus but turned back after grasping the truth that he was a revolutionary—though not the kind they may have expected. Jesus triggered an internal revolution of the spirit and soul that would result in transformed external behavior.

It wasn't public prayers, cosmetic fasting, or obsessive hand washing that proved a person's faith, said Jesus, but the fruit (see Matt. 7:16). In fact, genuine turning away from evil to God would be evidenced by fruit consistent with God's character (see Matt. 3:8).

Jesus preached not only this inside-out personal revolution but a bottom-up transformation of culture. The world would ultimately be ruled by the "meek," he said—those under discipline and control of the kingdom of heaven. The least in society's eyes would be the greatest in God's kingdom, not the pompous peacocks who strutted their pietism in the temple.

This was too much for culture-bound people who thought they wanted to follow Jesus.

Fear

"Tonight all of you will desert me," Jesus said as he ate the Passover meal with his disciples. The disciples were aghast and began pledging their undying loyalty.

"God will strike the Shepherd, and the sheep of the flock will be scattered," said Jesus, paraphrasing Zechariah 13:7.

Still his followers pledged themselves. Yet at the first clank of Roman armor, they sped away from him in fear for their lives.

Disagreement with His Vision, Mission, Goals, and Strategies

Jesus' vision was of a world restored to the Father and in perfect relationship with him. Many people wanted that—even some of Jesus' opponents.

But when Jesus' mission to achieve that vision is presented, small tornadoes are whipped up by furiously scampering feet. The notion of the cross and its gore is too much. The idea that they would have to class themselves as "sinners" and turn away from favorite indulgences is more than the quitters can stomach. They leave quickly, looking for a guru who will give them paradise without the blood and let them keep their lifestyles.

A college professor whose lifestyle professed atheism surprised everyone by joining a church. The academic had strong political convictions, and he said openly he was linking with the church for political rather than theological reasons. He wanted to engage people in political discussion and seek to organize the church around his causes. "So I'm a Christian, sort of," he wrote in a column announcing his decision.[13]

But a person who is a "sort of" anything isn't likely to stay when the vision fails, the mission aborts, goals seem unattainable, and strategies appear not to work.

Discomfort with His Style

Jesus' direct mode of communication was a turnoff to some of his followers. He told them, "Unless you eat the flesh of the Son of Man and drink His blood, you have no life in yourselves" (John 6:53).

No doubt some of the disciples were able to understand Jesus' deeper meaning and knew he wasn't promoting cannibalism. Nevertheless, "Even his disciples said, 'This is very hard to understand. How can anyone accept it?'" (v. 60 NLT). At that point, "many of his disciples turned away and deserted him" (v. 66 NLT). They couldn't stomach Jesus' style of speech.

Distraction

A fabulously wealthy member of the elite asked Jesus how he could be assured of eternal life (see Luke 18:18). Jesus reminded the rich man of the commandments. "The man replied, 'I've obeyed all these commandments since I was a child'" (v. 21 NLT).

Jesus went to the core: the man's attitude about his wealth. "Sell all you have and give the money to the poor, and you will have treasure in heaven. Then come, follow me" (v. 22 NLT). The young man became sad and turned away from Jesus "because he was very rich" (v. 23 NLT). Affluence had its grip on the man.

Three important lessons emerge here. First, potential quitters must be confronted with the matters that distract them. Second, they should be challenged to get rid of the distractions. Third, they are to be called to the true course. In short, confront them, challenge them, and call them.

The Fear He Was on a Course of Failure

There was a paring down of the numbers who followed Jesus as more and more caught on that he was serious about going to Jerusalem, where execution awaited him.

A growing number considered Jesus a loser. How could success come to anyone who suggested it was hard for the rich to enter the kingdom of God, or that people would have to put Jesus above parents, properties, and purses? This message of his was so contrary to human nature no one would buy it. Better to silence Jesus and move him off history's stage. The ruckus Jesus was causing wasn't worth the bother.

Quitters concluded Jesus was on a road to nowhere, and they wanted to go somewhere—anywhere that would meet their self-expectations and load their larders.

It's Time for a Refill

When the quitter walks out and you want to yell, "Good riddance!"

Clara always knew more than I (Shaun)—or at least she gave that impression. She had been a volunteer in our youth ministry for two years before I arrived. "Now that you're our youth pastor, I'm going to stick around to make sure you do things the way they need to be done," she told me. I valued her insight and experience with the ministry I was seeking to lead.

Clara, however, fell into a spell of negativity. If I wanted to put the students at tables, she thought they would do better grouped on the floor. If I decided to add a game activity to a teaching session, she protested it would detract from "deeper things."

One day Clara came to see me. "I'm going away for a vacation. Do you think the ministry will be okay while I'm gone?" she asked.

That added the last fragment of chip to my shoulder. "The ministry will be just fine without you!" I said rudely.

Clara never returned as a volunteer. At first I was happy about that, but after a few months I reflected on the sharp way I had spoken to her. She was an important part of our ministry, but I had allowed her to drain me to the point that I had unwittingly pushed her into quitting.

When you want to leave with the quitters.

Have you ever looked with envy at people who were leaving your organization? You probably feel like a sailor on a sinking boat. Strong swimmers are splashing into the water, heading for shore. And there you sit, baling frantically and trying to keep the thing afloat.

In 1973, I (Wallace) struggled with this as I said goodbye to my friend, boss, and political mentor, Harry Dent, who left the Nixon administration to return to private life. I was so drained I wanted to walk out the White House door with Harry. But I had assignments to complete, and it was impossible to leave Washington at that point.

You are truly drained when you look wistfully at the exits.

When you lose your passion to convince the quitters to stay.

When you hear yourself saying, "I don't blame you for leaving," your emotional energy is just about depleted.

Maybe you heard the old joke about the man whose wife shook him awake on a Sunday morning. "Honey," she said, "it's time to get ready for church."

"I'm not going," he mumbled. "I hate the choir, the building is always too hot, the people are unfriendly, and the preaching is lousy."

"But dear, you must go. You're the pastor!"

Drained leaders don't care whether people stay on board or jump ship. In fact, their passion is so sapped they want to leave too.

Dealing with Quitters

Help Quitters Develop Character

Ralph Waldo Emerson said, "The characteristic of heroism is its persistency." All of us, he wrote, "have wandering impulses, fits and starts of generosity." But the important thing is "when you have chosen your part, abide by it, and do not weakly try to reconcile yourself with the world."[14]

The ability to resist that wandering urge and to become a person known for faithfulness rather than fits and starts is an issue of character. Good leaders who really care about their followers help them develop the character to stay in place, even when the heat's on. They do this by remaining steady themselves and providing a model of persistency. When Jesus might have turned and run into the darkness that night in Gethsemane, the disciples watched as he held his ground.

Challenge Quitters to Remember Why They Signed On

Effective leaders take their teams to the mountain periodically.

One day after long, grueling hours of ministry, Jesus took his disciples farther up the slopes. There, on what history would call "the hill of Beatitudes," Jesus laid out the principles of the kingdom of heaven.

He was getting the disciples up high enough they could get a larger perspective of himself and his kingdom—the reasons they had left their nets, houses, families, farms, and fortunes to follow. Down in the grit and grime of demons, sicknesses, dysfunctional people, and threatening situations, it was easy to forget the reasons and to think about quitting.

But up on the mountain, the whole scene is spread out below. When you remember why you signed on, the urge to quit flickers out.

Help Quitters See Where They Fit in the Big Picture

Cal was a volunteer in our (Shaun) student ministry some years ago. Within weeks of joining our church, he approached me about serving. I was excited because I had watched him connect well with the youth. Cal was also a gifted communicator, and we needed him.

Cal's drawback was that he had very low self-esteem. Nevertheless, one day I asked if he would teach a Wednesday night discipleship class for our young people.

"Shaun, I'm honored you would ask," he said. "Yes, I'd love to do that!"

"Why don't you start in two weeks? That'll give you time to study the materials," I replied.

Two days later, Cal phoned me. "Shaun, I just don't think I have what it takes. I'm not even sure I'm volunteer material."

I knew something deeper was going on. "Cal, Satan is trying to make you ineffective. I've seen how you relate to students, and you'll be great."

"I'm just not sure," he said. "Let me pray about it some more."

A couple of days later, Cal phoned again. "Okay, I think I'm ready. I'm actually excited about teaching and volunteering in other ways in the youth ministry."

But a week later, Cal was sitting in my office. "I'm thinking of quitting the student ministry," he told me. "I just don't have what it takes."

"Cal, God has gifted you to work with young people," I replied, "and Satan hates that. The devil will do all possible to make you feel like you're worthless and a failure. I don't want to press you into doing something you can't do, but I believe God has given you what you need for the task."

Cal nodded. "You're right. I'll teach the class, Shaun."

Cal was nervous the first Wednesday night. However, about eight minutes into his presentation, something clicked. He broke the ice with a joke the young people loved. Then Cal got into his groove, and the session flowed.

I watched Cal over a period of months. His teaching and other gifts developed. I was so glad I had dug in and hadn't let him quit. Cal had been focused on his own perceptions of his limited abilities. When he got the longer view of what

God could do through him, Cal's sense of self-esteem and his confidence improved.

Don't Quit the Quitter

Earlier we wrote of John Mark, who quit Paul and Barnabas on the way to preach to the Gentiles. But the story didn't end there.

Late in his ministry, Paul wrote to Timothy, "Please come as soon as you can. Demas has deserted me because he loves the things of this life and has gone to Thessalonica. Crescens has gone to Galatia, and Titus has gone to Dalmatia" (2 Tim. 4:9–10 NLT). Now it was just Paul and Luke. But Paul needed someone else. He asked Timothy to bring Mark with him, "for he is profitable to me for the ministry" (v. 11 KJV). The man who had been a liability is now profitable!

The implications are huge. Barnabas never gave up on John Mark. Because of Barnabas's persistent training and encouragement of John Mark, Paul himself benefited at a crucial season in his ministry.

Do all possible not to quit the quitters who drain you. The day may come when they are the people who help fill your tank.

19

STRIDE BREAKERS

Stride breakers drain you by trying to get you to run with their rhythm and pace.

Distracters pull you off your path. Under the influence of the stride breakers, you don't leave the path, but your progress is stymied.

"Don't ever look back at the other runners!" was the command of my (Shaun) high school track coach. *Just looking out the corner of my eye at the competition can't slow me down*, I thought one day. I glanced into the other lane and slowed just enough to throw me off the pace and out of the winner's circle.

I was my own worst enemy.

The principle that works in sports is applicable in all life relationships and endeavors. Stride breakers can upset the pace of your marriage, parenting, group leading, work, and anything else you do.

I (Wallace) learned important lessons about stride breaking from my dog Charlie, a fifty-pound mix between a Labrador retriever and a Bluetick hound. Charlie is my jogging partner. Running with her on the dirt road beside our small Texas ranch has been a schooling in stride.

I have noted there are several phenomena that break Charlie's stride and could affect you also in similar ways.

Animals

A rabbit is a distracter, but another dog is a stride breaker for Charlie. Copper, for example, is an energetic collie who often runs parallel to Charlie and me, but she is inside the fence on the neighboring farm. Charlie and I are out on the open road, but Copper teases her and slows her down.

Copper is to Charlie what other human runners are to a person in a race. They can break a winning stride by alluring a racer to change his or her stride to match theirs.

Odors

Deer hiding over in a stand of trees, a skittish skunk, or some other smell will cause Charlie to lose attention and change her stride.

For humans, the "odors" are the promises of intrigue in running with a different gait. They pull at us to not run so fast in our pursuit of God and his kingdom. "You're becoming a fanatic" may be the charge others level at us to slow us down.

Then there is the fragrance of "Babylon," the fallen world system. It twirls around our nostrils, threatening to completely halt our forward motion.

Resist the "odors" that stop you in your tracks.

The Rear View

The other day, Charlie got hung up on the rear view. Another dog walking with its owner passed us by, going the opposite direction. Charlie was leashed at my side and didn't give chase, but she kept looking back wistfully.

For us, there are two forms of looking back that slow our stride—glorying or grieving.

Stride breakers may tempt you to keep your focus on a previous lap when you ran a winning pace. But gazing at the past stride that might have brought you victory and glory will keep you from winning the current race.

Similarly, grieving over past mistakes has kept many a runner from finishing the race, but not John Stephen Akhwari. The marathon at the 1968 Olympics had been won an hour before, but Tanzania's Akhwari still jogged into the Mexico stadium. Blood was seeping from his bandaged leg, the result of a painful fall out on the twenty-six-mile course.

Akhwari, lamed by his accident, limped around the Olympic track. Spectators stood and began to applaud.

"Why didn't you give up?" an observer asked.

"My country didn't send me seven thousand miles to start this race," said Akhwari. "My country sent me to finish."[1]

Don't allow the rear view to slow your gait, whether it's relishing past glories or lamenting earlier falls.

The Stride-Breaking Drain

Stride breakers batter you with a storm of words, set of agendas, and speed of pace that mess up your game, foul your plans, hinder your goals, thwart your mission, dry up your vision, and trip you in the pursuit. In short, they are drainers.

Some years ago I (Wallace) dealt with these drainers as I consulted with a government agency making dramatic changes in organization and management. The chief executive gave me two directives. He wanted a shift to faith-based values that would soak into every one of the agency's six hundred employees, and he desired the revolution to be bottom-up, employee driven.

God gave me what the King James Bible calls a "witty invention" (see Prov. 8:12). A strategy emerged, the boss approved, and we were on our way. It took six months, but a change of pace developed throughout the agency.

There were, however, two stride breakers, both top-line executives in charge of crucial departments. If the whole institution was going to change, it had to move at a carefully clocked pace. But the two stride breakers had their own running rates.

Mr. Fox was an old salt convinced he could take his unit on a faster run into transition. Mr. Tortoise was also a seasoned veteran, but he hated change and tried to slow and even halt the pace.

It took an executive order from the top boss to get these two men in stride. Their employees were losing out, and their attitudes were confusing the pack.

The stride breakers are everywhere, not just in businesses and government agencies. Paul says life is a race and the goal is to win (see 1 Cor. 9:24). For eternity, the gold at the end of the marathon is unceasing life in the manifest presence of God—heaven. In the material world, the prize is being alive with the fullness of Christ through his Holy Spirit and through conformity to his character.

To run effectively requires endurance, or staying power (see Heb. 12:1). If you're five foot eight, as I (Wallace) am, and you try to set your stride at the pace of an NBA center, your endurance will wear out. On the other hand, if you take up the stride of a toddler, you'll lose your endurance through sheer boredom.

Jesus and the Stride Breakers

As we've seen in other chapters, there were times Jesus' biological family could have been serious drainers.

It began early. There are many things that happened in Jesus' life on earth that didn't get written down (see John 21:25). We have only one cameo from Jesus' childhood—his trip to Jerusalem and the temple with Mary and Joseph when Jesus was twelve.

In giving us that snippet of the young Jesus, the Bible shows that the man who ran the race all the way was already on pace as a boy. Right there at the start, Jesus confronted stride breakers in Mary and Joseph.

Somewhere on the trek, they lost the boy. Mary and Joseph searched three days, finally locating him with religious leaders in the temple.

> "Son!" his mother said to him. "Why have you done this to us? Your father and I have been frantic, searching for you everywhere."
>
> "But why did you need to search?" he asked. "You should have known that I would be in my Father's house."
>
> Luke 2:48–49 NLT

The stride was struck, and Jesus wouldn't be pulled from it, even as a child.

Ultimately his blood kin would catch up, but they couldn't keep pace with Jesus and tried to slow him to their own gait. So years later—this time concerned for his mental well-being—they tried to pull Jesus to their stride.

Jesus was grappling with scribes and Pharisees when someone interrupted him.

> "Your mother and your brothers are outside, and they want to speak to you."
>
> Jesus asked, "Who is my mother? Who are my brothers?" Then he pointed to his disciples and said, "These are my mother and brothers. Anyone who does the will of my Father in heaven is my brother and sister and mother!"
>
> Matthew 12:47–50 NLT

Jesus wasn't rejecting his own kin but was speaking of stride. Those who run the race with him, at his side, constitute his band of brothers and sisters.

It's Time for a Refill

When you want someone else to set the pace.

Speed skating is one of the most demanding competitions of the Winter Olympics. In a long race, the lead may swap many times. Occasionally, faster racers will drop back so they can conserve energy for the last lap.

If you drop back because you've lost your passion to lead, the stride breakers are getting to you. If it's necessary to step back, do so only to gather your energies to lead again.

Rudolph Giuliani, mayor of New York when the World Trade Center collapsed on September 11, 2001, described his last day in office. After attending his successor's swearing in, Giuliani visited Ground Zero. The visit sparked his anger concerning the terrorist attack that took place there, but Giuliani wrote later, "The challenge was to put it [the energy behind his anger] to work in ways that would make a stronger, better leader."[2] Giuliani's attitude was he was moving off point, but only for the sake of readying for the next leadership mission.

When you trip over your own feet because you're focusing on a new pacesetter.

When I (Shaun) arrived at Saddleback Church, I was aware of the huge privilege of serving under Pastor Rick Warren and his team. Among the greatest challenges was following Doug Fields, my predecessor.

I soon discovered I was my own stride breaker, tripping myself. Encouragement was all I ever received from Doug, yet I was pressuring myself into an unsuitable stride. At last I settled into the right stride as I realized I was called to run not at Doug's pace but at that suited to me and to my gifts, talents, and personality.

Dealing with Stride Breakers

Keep Your Eyes on the Goal

The key to Jesus' amazing ability to run a race that included the horrible "lap" of the cross was to focus on his goal.

Hebrews 12:2 says, "For the joy set before Him [He] endured the cross." The joy was his goal, fulfilling his Father's will, and making it possible for human beings to be restored to the Father.

We are to run the race with the goal in mind, looking to Jesus' example all the way. He sets a stride with which we can win the race, because he supplies the energy through his Holy Spirit.

I (Wallace) counseled Betty, a young woman who was blossoming under the fresh work of Christ in her life but seemed off pace.

"I have realized just this morning what a deep root of bitterness I have toward my ex-husband," she told me. "I honestly feel hatred toward him. I'm ready to submit to God, and though I'm too weak in my own power I know he'll give me the power to truly forgive him. I want to completely eradicate the bitterness I have and move on to a fuller awareness of the Lord. I know God will reveal to me what I'm to do when I seek him in his Word."

Betty was being pulled off stride by a hurtful past, but the moment she told me of her determination to look to God and his Word rather than her pained emotions and memories, I knew she would get back in the race and in stride. And she did!

Know Your Own Stride

There are three ways you know your personal stride.

First, understand your spiritual gifts, the supernatural capacities God grants to do his work through you. No single person has all the gifts described in the Bible. The church is the body of Christ. *All* the gifts are in him and actualized in his people through the Holy Spirit. The diversity of gifts throughout the body means it takes the whole community of faith working together to minister the wholeness of Jesus.

When we forget this truth, we lose sight of others in the church and their gifts, and we fail to understand our own unique "stride." We are tempted to become a one-person show, playing all the roles and performing all the tasks.

This happened to me as a college student studying for the ministry. I had not identified my own spiritual gifts, instead focusing on those of some of my heroes. Initially I tried to mimic their style, even their dress. But as I discovered my spiritual gifts, I found the stride at which God designed me to run.

Second, understand the talents God has given you. Spiritual gifts are supernatural abilities, but talents are your natural strengths. When you desire talents you see in others and become frustrated because your natural abilities seem not to measure up to theirs, you will lose stride.

Third, "know thyself." That means understanding who you are—your personality type. As noted in chapter 14, spiritual gifts and talents are the components for your life's purpose, and personality is the container.

By understanding how spiritual gifts, talents, and personality work in your life, you will find your stride and settle into it.

Be Willing to Stretch

Finding your own stride doesn't mean an unwillingness to stretch it. Growth means enlarging your abilities within the giftedness, talents, and personality God has given you. You're running at your pace but quickening it and expanding your stride.

Ed Young, pastor of Houston's Second Baptist Church, where I (Wallace) serve, constantly seeks to stretch his stride. As I write, Dr. Young has been Second's pastor for twenty-seven years. When he arrived, the church's attendance was four to five hundred. Second now has forty-two thousand members on five campuses.

One of the keys to Dr. Young's success is his ability to maintain pace and, at the same time, continually lengthen stride. He is the most focused leader I've ever served under and a constant learner.

God has used Dr. Young's settled stride to keep the church stable, yet the pastor's careful stretching makes the huge church flexible in reaching thousands of people with Christ's transforming message.

Encourage Others to Stay on Stride

In a baseball game, Phil Rizzuto trotted out to his field position in the top of the ninth inning, with his Yankees behind 9-0. Before the opposing team came to bat, Rizzuto turned away momentarily from the batter's box, too dejected to look.

He caught sight of Joe DiMaggio in center field. Immediately Rizzuto said, "We're going to win this game." DiMaggio was the symbol of victory, and all it took was his presence to keep his team on stride to victory.[3]

Run the Whole Race with the End in Mind

In his book *Good to Great*, Jim Collins tells of the coaching staff of a high school cross-country team who met for dinner after winning their second state championship in two years.

"I don't get it," said one of the coaches. "Why are we so successful? We don't work any harder than other teams. And what we do is so simple. Why does it work?"

The coaches found their runners ran best at the end of workouts, races, and the season, when it counted the most. They geared to the simple idea, "We run best at the end," and the coaching staff knew how to create this effect better than any other team in the state.

The students learned how to pace themselves and race with confidence. "We run best at the end," they think at the end of a hard race. "So, if I'm hurting bad, then my competitors must hurt a whole lot worse!"[4]

Jesus shows if we refuse to be pulled off stride—no matter what other runners are doing, no matter the intrigues that pull at us, no matter how much the past tries to slow us down—we will win the gold. His kingdom, still advancing on the earth after twenty centuries, proves it.

20

WHINERS

Whiners drain you with their constant woes, unceasing dissatisfactions, and endless gripes.

Usually, complainers are focused on specifics—the way you led in a certain situation, the temperature of the room, or the makeup of the team. Whining, on the other hand, tends to be a state of being. You can often satisfy the complainer by correcting the specific source of concern, but the whiners seldom seem satisfied no matter what you do.

The Whining Drain

"Dan Despondent" was a member of the first church I (Shaun) served. He appeared at almost every meeting with a bellyache. He moaned about the church's water bill in one session.

"But that car wash raised a lot of money to send students on the youth mission trip," replied one of the elders.

Dan retorted, "We shouldn't be sending kids to help people in other places when we've got so much need around here!"

On another occasion he said, "We're not being good stewards of our money. We keep running all this air conditioning. Turn up the thermostat a notch or two. My wife and I have learned to cope with the heat at home, and the church can too!"

Eventually Dan lost his credibility with the church leadership. No one paid attention to him. It's no surprise the world is full of people like Dan, since 80 percent of what people take in is negative, and, according to one poll, 90 percent of Americans are in chronic stress.[1]

Despite efforts to improve job environments, writes Michelle Malkin, "we remain a slackening nation of work-avoidance wimps and moaning mollycoddles."[2] Malkin may be overstating the case, but anyone seeking to work with people or lead an organization has met whiners.

Jesus and the Whiners

"Moaning mollycoddles" might well describe many in the mobs Jesus met.

God sent John the Baptist to put the final milepost of the old covenant beside the road. Now, John had a different style and appearance than that of Jesus, and people whined about his manner. "He's too coarse; he smells like a camel; he has no communication skills; he isolates himself too much; there's no mercy in him," they might have said.

Then Jesus came, displacing John and crossing the border between the old covenant and the new. The whiners still tagged along, murmuring, "He associates with sinners; he drinks wine and goes to feasts and parties; he doesn't fast like John the Baptist."

And that brought Jesus to observe,

How shall I describe this generation? These people are like a group of children playing a game in the public square. They complain to their friends, "We played wedding songs, and you weren't happy, so we played funeral songs, but you weren't sad." For John the Baptist didn't drink wine and he often fasted, and you say, "He's demon possessed." And I, the Son of Man, feast and drink, and you say, "He's a glutton and a drunkard, and a friend of the worst sort of sinners!" But wisdom is shown to be right by what results from it.

Matthew 11:16–19 NLT

Jesus noted that whiners are never satisfied. Change your vision, rewrite your mission, alter your goals, and shift your strategies, and they will moan you are unstable, unsteady, and too given to change.

Jesus shows that you should ignore the whiners, press on with your strategic plan, and let the results speak for themselves.

It's Time for a Refill

When you start leading with your emotions.

When the whiners drive you to distraction, the emotions take over, and you start thrashing rather than leading.

Deep in the wilderness of Zin, Moses finally has had it with the whiners. On the tedious, torturous path out of Egypt, they've drained him until there's only a drop or two of faith and patience in his tank.

Now they come bellyaching about the water.

The people blamed Moses and said, "We wish we had died in the LORD's presence with our brothers! Did you bring the LORD's people into this wilderness to die, along with all our livestock? Why did you make us leave Egypt and bring us here to this terrible place? This land has no grain, figs, grapes, or pomegranates. And there is no water to drink!"

Numbers 20:3–5 NLT

Running into the tabernacle tent they've pitched in the wilderness, Moses and Aaron fall on their faces before God, who tells Moses, "You and Aaron must take the staff and assemble the entire community. As the people watch, command the rock over there to pour out its water. You will get enough water from the rock to satisfy all the people and their livestock" (v. 8 NLT).

Moses fetches the staff and heads for the rock. But in the face of all the whiners, rather than speaking to the rock, the leader of Israel starts thrashing at it with the wooden staff. Water pours out, but not according to God's plan. That snit costs Moses the privilege of leading Israel into the Promised Land.

Don't let the whiners drive you to distraction so that your emotions rule you. If you're being tempted to strike rather than speak, recognize how drained you are. Pull back until you recover your inner strength. Otherwise you will squander your leadership.

When you want to throttle rather than coddle.

I (Wallace) understand the urge to throttle a whiner. Years ago, I was approached by a man who'd heard I was the son of an alcoholic. "You can relate to me," he said. "I have a lot of bitterness because of my dad, and I want to get over my anger."

I embraced this brother, full of compassion for a man struggling with the same issues I'd battled. God had shown me the way out of that misery, and I felt confident that, through Christ, I could help the wounded man.

In session after session, he recited formalized characteristics of those who had grown up in an alcoholic home.

The profile had been sketched out by a group focusing on adult children of alcoholics (ACOA).

"I am an ACOA," he said every time we met.

"No, you're not!" I would answer. "You told me you've received Christ. The Bible says that in him you are a 'new creation,' and that the past with all its old garbage has gone away" (see 2 Cor. 5:17). That discovery had transformed my life, and I desperately wanted my friend to understand it.

But week after week, he kept whining. Rather than talking about what it meant to be a new creature in Christ, he wanted to go back over the old hurts one more time.

I knew when his whining had just about emptied me. Rather than coddling him, I wanted to throttle him. I was tempted to turn my hug into a hammerlock. I had to pull away from him until my consternation was converted back to compassion.

When you've moved from Happy Valley to the Great Dismal Swamp.

In the Hebrew of the Old Testament, *garden* means "hedged-in place." Its boundaries prevent the entry of evil. Breach the bush, and all sorts of things come in. Like a whining spirit.

Blame is a favorite activity of whiners. Adam eats the forbidden fruit, is found out by God, and says, "The woman whom *You* gave to be with me, *she* gave me from the tree, and I ate" (Gen. 3:12, italics added). Adam gives the blame to God and Eve. Now he is behaving like his new daddy, the devil, by being an accuser. The garden is violated, the jungle snakes into Paradise, and Happy Valley becomes the Great Dismal Swamp.

Leadership expert Danny Cox describes the ten characteristics that classify the whiners:

1. Uncooperative attitudes
2. Lack of enthusiasm
3. Absence of commitment
4. Fault finding
5. Increasing complaints
6. Growing tardiness and absenteeism
7. Deterioration in the appearance of the work area
8. Breakdown in discipline
9. Long faces
10. Low morale as a rallying point[3]

If you see your "garden" full of these slithering elements, find the gaps in the hedge and close them in a hurry, lest whiners start popping out of the ground like summer weeds.

Dealing with Whiners

Deal with Specific Complaints

Your best people complain occasionally. Don't write them off as whiners.

"I've been struggling with allergies," Rae said when she met with Alice, her supervisor. "I also noticed several others in our work area getting sick, and I think we found the problem."

Alice leaned forward, eager to listen.

"The drapes on the big windows surrounding our work stations haven't been cleaned in a year," Rae continued. "They're full of dust and mites. That's what's making us sick."

Alice had a choice. She could categorize Rae as a whiner or take seriously her complaint of dusty drapes. Alice had never heard anything from Rae but positive and constructive words. She knew there was a real problem to address. She phoned her facilities office immediately and ordered the curtains cleaned.

Be careful not to lump complainers and whiners in the same bunch. You may need to hear and act upon specific concerns when people complain.

Ignore the Whine and Encourage the Song

Don't fret over whining. My (Shaun) son is passing through the whiner stage. "Dad, you're making me late," he moaned as we drove to baseball practice. "The coach is really going to be mad at me."

I kept driving, silent.

"I can't get my cleats tied," I heard from the backseat. "It's your fault because you didn't help me put on my shoes before we got in the car."

I was mum as a rock.

Austin is eight years old and will grow out of the whining stage because I don't coddle him. Children allowed to cope with life by manipulating others become adults who whine in the workplace, at church, in their marriages, and in every other arena of life.

Instead of responding to the whine, encourage the song. Set a rule, operating procedure, or expectation that for every whine there must be the recounting of two blessings. Every time the whiners in your circle begin their laments, let them know they must pay the "price" of reporting on two blessings they've received recently before you will listen to the latest misery.

After awhile, the hymn displaces the dirge.

Don't Engage with Whiners

"Don't ask open-ended questions [of whiners], not even 'How are you?'" That advice came from folks dealing with draining people in the workplace. The writers suggest limiting greetings to "Good morning" and "Good evening." Further, "The words, 'I'm sorry, I don't have time to chat right now' are your friends. Know them, love them, use them."[4]

Such advice seems cold and insensitive, especially to people driven by mercy, compassion, and a desire to encourage others. But it's important to face the hard truth that sometimes we *enable* people to be whiners when we turn on their faucets with open-ended conversations.

Jesus encountered people with whom he wouldn't engage. Rather than attempting to rebut the crowds whining about the perceived injuries he had brought their cherished belief system, Jesus was silent. To answer would have opened the spigot wider, causing more carping accusation to pour out.

I (Shaun) once dealt with a parent who was the poster child of whining. I worked hard to appease her—which only resulted in more whining followed by more appeasement—until I was drained.

Once I taught a series of lessons about the danger of double-standard living. "That's not what the kids need to hear," she moaned. "I know, because my child isn't struggling with that kind of problem."

I was young and hadn't learned about the importance of not enabling the whiners, so I altered my series. Later Mrs. Whiner's teen said, "Shaun, I'm really struggling with living one way at church and another way at school."

The Lord had been leading me all along, but I allowed the whiner to get me off track. Biblically shaped leaders know the difference between being an enabler and an encourager. They discern the nature of individuals and give them what they need rather than what they want.

What the whiner may need is your silence.

Establish Whining as a Taboo

If a garden is a hedged-in place, there must be a strong fence set specifically to keep out whining.

JoAnna Brandi writes,

One whiner in the group can bring everyone down. A whiner is like an infection—it spreads. Put one strong whiner in a room and they can turn it into a pity party. Stop it at the source. Learn to spot them during the interview process. Don't hire them in the first place, unless you are prepared to keep vigilance over their behavior and attempt to change it. Good luck. Whiners love whining. Put a "No whining" sign on your door.[5]

Whining was excluded from Jesus' team. "I want to follow you, but first I have to bury my father," said one (see Matt. 8:21). Jesus replied, "Follow Me, and allow the dead to bury their own dead" (v. 22).

Once again, Jesus was being not insensitive but insightful. Burying the dead didn't necessarily mean the elderly person was deceased but rather was in old age, approaching death. To join Jesus' team meant utter focus and commitment, not whining about having to go home to handle personal issues.

Create a Positive World

Jesus brought people living in negative environments into a "can do" world of unlimited possibility, so it was hard to be a whiner in his kingdom.

He promised transformation. Unlettered fishermen (Peter and Andrew), corrupt politicians (Levi and Zacchaeus), misinformed intellectuals (Thomas), average Joes (Nathanael), and fiery zealots (James and John) could be made into ministers of God and transform the world.

Jesus encouraged them with the mountain-moving strength of faith. People who seemed not to be able to dislodge the Roman oppressors could, with faith, hurl a peak into the sea.

Jesus taught his followers the power of lifted eyes. "Look up!" was his constant, unspoken admonishment. "Look up to God and look out on the fields of need." By keeping their eyes on the Lord, they could feed the multitudes and bring in the rich harvest of more transformed lives.

Paul came to the pinnacle of this positive world Jesus created when he shouted from his prison cell, "I can do all things through [Christ] who strengthens me" (Phil. 4:13).

Whether you're a parent, boss, coach, teacher, or someone else who tries to lead people, think about the way you speak, the tone you set. Loving whiners means bringing them into an atmosphere where whining shrinks and dies.

Let Jesus Christ create his kingdom of righteousness, peace, and Spirit-ignited joy in you (see Rom. 14:17), and he will use you to bring others—including the whiners—into that wonderful world.

21

WOUNDERS

The wounders drain you with pain.

I (Shaun) know, because I was such a wounder. One day as a junior high kid I shot a verbal arrow straight into my mother's heart. I wanted to go to a friend's house after school, but my mom forbade it. My anger sizzled and I wanted to hurt her.

"Shaun, I need you to go to the grocery store with me," she said after arriving home from a long day at work. She needed me to help her handle bulky sacks.

"I don't want to," I answered. Occasionally my mother let me know without hesitation I would do what she ordered. This was one of those times. I rode in the car, but I refused to speak to her.

"Shaun, I didn't want you to go to Chris's house because you needed to get your homework done," she said as we headed to the store. "I have good reasons for the things I ask you to do, and you need to trust me."

I was silent.

"I love you," she said.

"I hate you," I shot back.

Instantly such pain clouded her face that I thought we might wreck. She pulled over. "Get out of the car," Mom said.

"But Mom, I was only kidding," I replied, trying to laugh.

"You don't kid like that. Now get out."

I leaped out, crying hysterically. I stood beside the road and watched her pull away, contemplating the sting I had brought her heart. I realized the arrow I had fired at her had ricocheted. I was drained by my own dart.

In less than a minute, my mother turned back around and pulled beside me. She let me back in the car. "Nothing has ever hurt me quite like you saying you hate me," she said that night. "Shaun, never forget the capacity we humans have to wound one another."

One of the most important things I learned that afternoon was how quickly and easily we thoughtlessly give pain to others.

The Proliferation of the Wounders

"Sixty-Five Percent in Test Blindly Obey Order to Inflict Pain," announced the *New York Times* on October 26, 1961. The discovery was sensational and shocking.

Stanley Milgram, a twenty-eight-year-old Yale Ph.D. in social psychology, decided to find out the extent to which people would comply with orders, even if it meant wounding others. Subjects were told they were participating in a study to discover how punishment related to learning. The researcher told participants to zap a "student" with an electrical machine whenever the "pupil" erred on an assigned task. With every mistake, the participants were told the voltage would be increased in increments of 15, all the way to 450 volts.

The subjects didn't know the electric box was a fake and the "student" was an actor. Nevertheless, the majority obeyed to the point they thought they were administering 450 volts to the actor who feigned pain.

The finding was distressing. It seemed that "an average, presumably normal group of New Haven, Connecticut, residents would readily inflict very painful and perhaps even harmful electric shocks on innocent victims."[1]

Part of what motivated Milgram, a Jew, was trying to understand how the Holocaust could have happened.

Hannah Arendt, an American political philosopher, pursued the same question. She had been born into a secular Jewish home in Germany but escaped to the United States in 1941. Two decades later, Arendt covered the trial in Israel of Adolf Eichmann—a prime Nazi leader who helped Hitler carry out the Holocaust—for the *New Yorker*. Four days after Milgram's shock experiments were concluded, the Israelis hanged Eichmann.

From Arendt's experience she penned a book, *Eichmann in Jerusalem*, in which she spoke of "the banality of evil," words contained in the subtitle. The popular view was the Nazi murderers were psychopathic, bloodthirsty monsters. Yet as Arendt observed Eichmann and listened to his defense before the Israeli court, she was struck by his apparent moral neutrality. He seemed not to be anti-Semitic but ordinary.

The Holocaust, she wrote, was for Jews "quite literally the end of the world." But for Eichmann, it was nothing more than a job "with daily routine and its ups and downs."[2]

Wounders can desensitize themselves to the drain and pain they bring others in their social or professional environment. This has powerful implications for the workplace, teams, and even religious groups.

Milgram suggested people become wounders because they see it either as a requirement of their particular social structure or because they want to be identified with it—to be "part of the team." But Milgram's conclusion was limited at several crucial points. First, many become wounding drainers because *they* have been wounded. Loving the wounders in your organization may mean seeking to understand why they strike out at others and helping them deal with their own pain.

Second, some want to wound others when their own agendas and desires are thwarted. That night when my (Shaun) mother refused to let me go to my friend's house, my first impulse was to wound her. Such a pattern brought into adulthood could have brought pain into every group of which I became a part.

Finally, the core issue is "All have sinned and fall short of the glory of God" (Rom. 3:23). At the root of wounding behavior is sin—a departure from the loving, pure character of God. Dealing only with culture, authority figures, personal agendas, and past hurts is merely applying a Band-Aid until the crisis of the human heart is resolved.

In the way Jesus handled the wounding drain, we can learn important lessons about how we deal with those who bring hurt to our souls.

Jesus and the Wounders

Seven hundred years before the Messiah's appearing, Isaiah described him in a strange way:

> He is despised and rejected of men; a man of sorrows, and acquainted with grief: and we hid as it were our faces from him; he was despised, and we esteemed him not. Surely he hath borne our griefs, and carried our sorrows: yet we did esteem him stricken, smitten of God, and afflicted. But he was wounded for our transgressions, he was bruised for our iniquities: the chastisement of our peace was upon him; and with his stripes we are healed. All we like sheep have

gone astray; we have turned every one to his own way; and the LORD hath laid on him the iniquity of us all.

The world's Savior would be the wounded healer. Consider the extent of his wounds:

- **His feet were pierced.** A brawny Roman pounded large spikes through Jesus' feet, attaching them to the cross. Jesus' feet had transported him to needy people. Now his feet were paralyzed, impaled in the wood, and spilling out his blood.
- **His hands were wounded.** Jesus' hands had cradled babies and touched untouchable lepers. They had been stretched out over a stormy sea to bring it peace. His hands had hewn rough wood in Joseph's carpenter shop, and now they were one with the splintery wood, immobilized.
- **His heart was penetrated.** The heart of the world's Messiah had been moved with compassion for the shepherdless multitudes. That great heart had been united with the weary and fainting, the bleeding and dying. Now it poured water and blood into earth's soil, a cleansing rain that would heal others.
- **His mind was hurt.** Jesus' mind had reeled with the realization of his friends' betrayal, denial, and flight from him. But it got worse. Somewhere in that gruesome afternoon, his mind could not find his Father. That union had been his strength, and now he knew it was severed. The word "forsaken" floated through his brain and seeped from his lips.
- **His emotions were shattered.** There is no deeper wound to the soul than abandonment by those one cherishes. The Father's Son became living, breathing iniquity, for at that moment he was "made . . . to be

WOUNDERS

251

sin for us" (2 Cor. 5:21), and the absolutely Holy One cannot look upon absolute evil.

Christ knows "the feeling of our infirmities" (Heb. 4:15 KJV). And to some small measure, we feel his pain as well. Paul writes that we "fill up that which is behind of the afflictions of Christ" (Col. 1:24 KJV) in our work for and in his name.

It's Time for a Refill

When you no longer feel like walking toward the need.

Fred was a loving dad and wanted to do all possible to prepare Andy, his son, for his career. "Son, I want to give you some good advice," said Fred one day. "If you want to shine at work, find the problems and run straight toward them with a solution. Don't ever run away from them."

Years later, Andy became vice president of a company where a monstrous crisis loomed. Andy worked long hours devising a solution and asked Morris, his CEO, for an opportunity to speak at the next management team meeting.

The following Tuesday, Andy outlined his strategy for defusing the crisis. It would require a huge energy output from him and his staff, but he was willing to commit, he told the senior executives.

That Thursday the office scuttlebutt, Jerry, scampered into his office and said, "When you left the room the other day, Morris joked about you wanting to take over the whole company."

"But he thanked me and said the management team would get back to me right away," Andy said, bewildered.

"Get back to you?" Jerry replied, incredulous. "They think you're just trying to use this problem to advance your own ambitions. I wouldn't be surprised if they're trying to figure out how to send you to our office at the North Pole!"

Internally Andy was grimacing from the wound. He vowed never again to follow his father's advice. Andy's feet would stay in their place on terra firma—his office.

The wound had drained him of his desire to initiate contributive actions.

When your hands are hurting too badly to serve someone else.

Pianist Artur Schnabel was diagnosed with neuritis in his hands. It was an "occupational disease," he said.

Other famous concert players would have agreed. "Throughout my entire stay in Copenhagen, I always had to tolerate grief and anxiety concerning my fingers, which were constantly inflamed with much playing," wrote Clara Schumann in her diary. "I am very tired and my hands hurt," Sergei Rachmaninoff said in a letter.[3]

Those who seek to lead people by serving them may never touch a piano key, but they know what it means to have hands they have extended in kindness wounded so sharply they're tempted to draw them back.

When your energy is gushing out.

In 1737, John Wesley found himself where he did not want to be—in love.

He had come from England to evangelize the American colony of Georgia. At church there, Wesley met Sophia Christiana Hopkey, a delightful seventeen-year-old who showed up every morning for a prayer service. But Wesley was determined, in his own words, "to have no intimacy with any woman in America." He had come not to court but to convert, and he aimed to remain celibate.

Nevertheless, Sophy's aunt Mrs. Causton planted the notion Sophy would make a fine wife. But it wouldn't work, Wesley told himself. He was to be an itinerant missionary. A married man was tied down.

But Sophy had worked her way into his heart, and Wesley was miserable. He finally acknowledged to himself his love for her. But just as he faced the truth, rumor circulated that another man was after Sophy—William Williamson, for whom Wesley had little respect.

Wesley wrote in his diary he was "in the toils." Author John Pollock writes, "The more he saw Sophy, the more he loved her,"[4] and he knew he was losing his resolve not to marry.

As Wesley settled into the notion of wedding Sophy, he received a gashing wound. As Sophy's pastor, he was asked to publish the banns of marriage between her and Williamson. Sophia Hopkey and William Williamson were married a few days later.

Wesley reeled at that turn of events since Sophy had denied there was a courtship. He fell into "a complication of passions and tumult." Wesley paced his garden and later recorded his feelings: "Tried to pray, lost, sunk."[5]

John Wesley experienced what many have felt—the drain of the wounders.

When your capacity for rational thought is ebbing away.

Some years ago, I (Wallace) was building a deck behind our house. I was nailing a six-by-six post requiring hard hammer thrusts. Suddenly my thumb got in the way. The blow was so hard it nipped off a little corner of my thumb.

The pain rocketed into every member of my body and had me totally in its grip. I could think of nothing else. I struggled down from the ladder. My helper assisted me into the house, where my wife wrapped my hand in ice. I lay on my bed, unable to think, unable to move, drained by the pain.

There are emotional woundings that puncture us with such pain. When we hurt so badly we can think of nothing else, we are seriously depleted. It's time to pull back from the work and "ice" ourselves down. That means not only a physical withdrawal from our tasks but also a mental Sabbath from dwelling on the problem.

When the wounding of the spirit drains you of the light.

During the American Revolution, George Washington believed the West Point garrison to be "the most strategic location in the entire northern theater."[6] There Washington had stationed one of his most able leaders, Benedict Arnold. But to his great dismay, Washington found out Arnold was being bribed by the enemy to turn over West Point to them.

Washington's world darkened. "After all," writes author Joseph Ellis, "if Arnold could sell out, the prospects were dim indeed."[7] Washington faced a grim situation with the British winning in the southern colonies, his own army disintegrating, and the Continental Congress that had sent Washington into battle claiming "to be powerless to reverse the course by providing revenue."[8]

Then came Benedict Arnold's wound to Washington's heart. It was all the American leader could do to see a mere hint of light.

Such is the drain of the wounders.

Dealing with Wounders

Forgive the People Who Wounded You

Of all the words Jesus uttered from the cross, perhaps none were more surprising than "Father, forgive them; for they know not what they do" (Luke 23:34 KJV).

My (Wallace) words were also a surprise to Nancy. The thirty-something woman had come to tell me she had become a Christian. But there was a massive obstacle. "Don't ask me to forgive my father," she said. She described the pain her father had brought her through sexual abuse.

"Okay," I said, "but you must forgive your father."

"How can I do that?"

"God doesn't ask you to act out of your wounded emotions, but out of your will," I told her.

Nancy engaged her will, and one day a couple of years later, she beamed as she introduced me to her dad, who was attending church with her.

To forgive the wounders in your life, allow the will, not the emotions, to pull your train. The will must be the engine, and the emotions the caboose. I've never seen a train whose engine was a caboose and whose caboose was an engine. Yet that's the kind of train we try to build when we expect the wounded emotions to provide the power.

Forgiving your wounders will plug the big hole they've punched in your heart.

Do All Possible to Heal the Wounds of the Wounders

"Daddy, are you a werewolf?" my young daughter asked me one night as I (Shaun) tucked her in.

I chuckled, but I could remember a time such words would have wounded me. I was born with ears not formed correctly. Some called me "Spock," after the *Star Trek* character. Others said I looked like an elf, and that hurt even worse.

Eventually I grew out of being offended about my ears. That night I told my daughter, "No, I'm an elf, and Santa sent me here to watch little kids like you." We both laughed.

I also chuckled when Jackie, an awkward student in our youth ministry, said, "Pastor Shaun, I never noticed it before, but you have elf ears!"

Jackie is a wounder. She's always poking at people over their clothes, hair, or weight. But her words gave me no pain. I know why she has a compulsion to hurt others. Jackie is a social outcast. She's a young woman whose self-esteem is at the bottom of the Grand Canyon.

Like so many people, Jackie's a wounder because she's so wounded. As a leader who claims to follow the master leader and relater, I must not respond to her assaults with slicing retorts but must seek to heal Jackie's wounds by making her feel important to the group and its members.

This was what Jesus did for the repentant thief. Perhaps the man had been a reject all his life. But the Lord of glory told the dying man he had a place in God's paradise. For the first time ever, someone touched the deep pain that had caused him to wound others.

Understand the Pain Is Part of the Process

There was a pit in the path to Joseph's purpose. His own brothers were Joseph's draining wounders. Full of jealousy and stirred by his own immature actions, they hurled him into a cistern. There in the pit, Joseph sweated out his future.

Though he couldn't see it, a dust cloud arose on the horizon. A caravan of Egypt-bound traders approached. Joseph's brothers decided it would be better to make a buck over their bothersome sibling than to let him rot in the pit, so soon Joseph was headed for Egypt. Straight into his destiny.

God wastes nothing. Whatever comes into your life contributes to his purpose in and through you (see Rom. 8:28–29). And that includes your wounds.

Celebrate the Victory Brought by the Wounds

"*Tetelestai!* It is finished!" Jesus shouts. Not "*I* am finished!" but "*It* is finished!" Right there in the midst of the searing wounds and howling mobs, Jesus has a party. He celebrates the victory.

Tetelestai comes from another Greek term, *teleo*, meaning "purpose" and "the completion of a mission." Jesus' mission had been to reveal the Father, model the lifestyle of the kingdom of heaven, and atone for humanity's sin. His wounds were essential to the mission. After his resurrection, Jesus showed his scars to Thomas, not only to persuade his doubting friend but also to display the victory.

If you understand the wounds are the means to your success, you can forgive the draining wounder and celebrate, not as a masochist but as a victor. That is precisely how I (Wallace) was freed from bitterness and unforgiveness toward my dad.

As I noted earlier, my father was an alcoholic. I enshrined bitterness toward him in my soul for a long time. One day it occurred to me that, as Alan Paton reminds us in *Cry, the Beloved Country*, wounds heal wounds. God had seen my destiny before I was born and had foreseen my father's alcoholism and the pain it would bring. God didn't cause my father's problem, but in his foreknowledge he chose that dad for me. Why? So I could relate to the pain I would seek to help heal as a pastor.

When I understood that truth, I celebrated every tear, every disappointment, and every deep wound to my heart in those growing-up years. Compassion and forgiveness for my father flooded my heart. I was no longer drained but was filled to overflowing.

In the deepest way possible, I had come to love the drainer.

CONCLUSION

No matter what variety the drainers may be or where you encounter them, the call of Jesus to his people is always to love them. You may want to avoid them, sack them, or sock them, but Jesus leads you to something higher—unconditional love. Such love isn't based on how little or how much they sap you. It transforms them into real people with needs that drive their draining lifestyle.

God's love doesn't mean you enable the draining behavior in others. In fact, loving them may mean confronting the drainers with truth. God's love always involves a willful decision to help the drainers become contributors. Then you have the delight of standing back and watching the joy spread over a drainer's face when he or she blossoms into God's purpose!

NOTES

1. Abraham Lincoln, quoted in Andrew Carnegie, *Lincoln the Unknown* (Garden City, New York: Andrew Carnegie & Associates, 1959), 188.
2. Mark 10:45.

Introduction

1. Mark 5:34 authors' paraphrase.
2. Isaiah Berlin, quoted in Jim Collins, *Good to Great* (New York: Harper-Business, 2001), 90.
3. Jim Collins, *Good to Great* (New York: HarperBusiness, 2001), 91.
4. The most recent statistics can be found at www.haggai-institute .com.

Chapter 1: Angerers

1. Specific cases presented throughout the book are actual experiences or composites drawn from the authors' work and relationships. When a first name only appears, it is usually a fictitious name for a real person.
2. "Anger—How It Affects People," Better Health Channel, www .betterhealth.vic.gov.au/BHCV2/bhcarticles.nsf/pages/Anger_how_it _affects_people?open.
3. Frederick Buechner, *Wishful Thinking* (San Francisco: Harper, 1993), 117.

4. Pauline Wallin, "Get Mad? Get Even? Or . . ." *Inner Brat Newsletter*, 2002, www.drwallin.com/newsletter/pw-02-11.shtml.

Chapter 2: Chatterers

1. Marty Nemko, "Do You Talk Too Much?" homepage, www.martynemko.com/articles/do-you-talk-too-much_id1371.

2. Bruce Walker, "The Chattering Class Becomes the Stammering Class," Enter Stage Right, 2001, www.enterstageright.com/archive/articles/0801/0801stammer.htm.

Chapter 4: Confusers

1. "Cabinets & Vice Presidents," Mr. Lincoln's White House, 2005, www.mrlincolnswhitehouse.org/inside.asp?ID=9&subjectID=2.

2. Marilyn Gardner, "A Century of Conflicting Advice," *The Christian Science Monitor*, April 30, 2003, www.csmonitor.com/2003/0430/p14s01-lifp.htm.

3. Bruno Bettelheim, "Confused Parents, Confused Kids," *Time*, September 5, 1969, www.time.com/time/magazine/article/0,9171,901363,00 .html.

4. Richard Corliss, "That Old Feeling: Who Was Peter Sellers?" *Time*, February 10, 2003, www.time.com/columnist/corliss/article/0,9565, 421269,00.html.

Chapter 5: Critics

1. Sam Walton, *Made in America* (New York: Doubleday, 1992), 247–48.

2. Col. Mark Fentress, "Hold the Higher Ground in Both Military and Life," U.S. Army Corps of Engineers, March 4, 2004, www.hq.usace .army.mil/cepa/pubs/mar04/story3.htm.

3. "Judging and Serving," *Christian Today*, July 23, 2006, www.chris tiantoday.com/article/judging.and.serving/7009.htm

4. "Kindness," NeXt Bible™ Learning Environment, 2005, http://net .bible.org/illustration.php?topic=855.

5. Danny Cox with John Hoover, *Leadership When the Heat's On* (New York: McGraw-Hill, 1992), 113, italics in original.

6. Anthony D'Souza, *Developing the Leader Within You* (Singapore: Haggai Centre for Advanced Leadership Studies, 1994), 181.

7. Joe McKeever, homepage, "Katrina: Contradictions in Our Fair City," October 20, 2005, www.joemckeever.com/mt/archives/000174 .html.

Chapter 6: Cynics

1. Carter McNamara, "Overview of Cynicism in Business Organizations," Free Management Library, www.managementhelp.org/prsn_wll/cynicism.htm.
2. Ibid.
3. William Strauss, quoted in Wendy Murray Zoba, "The Class of '00 Part 2," *Christianity Today*, February 3, 1997, www.ctlibrary.com/ct/1997/february3/7t218a.html.
4. McNamara, "Overview."
5. Ibid.
6. "How Leaders Gain (and Lose) Confidence: An Interview with Rosabeth Moss Kanter," *Leader to Leader*, no. 35 (Winter 2005), www.pfdf.org/leaderbooks/l2l/winter2005/kanter.html.
7. Norman Gelb, *Ike and Monty* (New York: William Morrow and Company, 1994), 13.
8. Ibid., 14.

Chapter 7: Deceivers

1. Patrick Lencioni, *Five Dysfunctions of a Team* (San Francisco: Jossey-Bass, 2002), 195.
2. Ibid., 196.
3. Wallace Henley, *The White House Mystique* (Old Tappan, NJ: Fleming H. Revell, 1976).
4. Ibid., 33.
5. Peter F. Drucker, *Management* (New York: Harper & Row, 1973), 75.
6. Kern Lewis, review of *Kmart's Ten Deadly Sins*, by Marcia Layton Turner, Forbes.com, October 10, 2003, www.forbes.com/2003/10/10/1010kmartreview.html.
7. Ibid.
8. Mark Lander, "John McCain," The Vietnam War, April 26, 2000, www.vietnamwar.com/johnmccainbio.htm.

Chapter 8: Depressors

1. Dale Carnegie, *Lincoln the Unknown* (Garden City, New York: Dale Carnegie & Associates, 1959), 55.
2. Ibid.
3. Ibid.
4. Judith Briles, "Negative People Can Ruin a Good Attitude," *Denver Business Journal*, May 12, 2000, www.denver.bizjournals.com/denver/stories/2000/05/15/smallb4.html.

5. Ibid.

6. Peter Murphy, "Dealing with Negative People Made Easy," MAXX-MLM.com, 2005, www.e-comprofits.com/negativism.html.

7. Ibid.

Chapter 9: Disappointers

1. Rick Morrissey, "Fittingly, Bode Exits in a Blaze of Nothing," *Chicago Tribune Online Edition*, February 26, 2006, http://blogs.chicagotribune .com/news_columnists_ezorn/2006/02/index.html.

2. Billy Graham, *Just As I Am* (San Francisco: Harper/Zondervan, 1997), 457.

3. Stephen R. Covey, *Principle-Centered Leadership* (New York: Summit Books, 1991), 204–5.

4. Ibid.

5. Shawn Levy, "O Brother, Where Art Thou?" Guardian Unlimited, October 21, 2005, http://film.guardian.co.uk/print/0,,5314430-3181,00 .html.

6. "Mackenzie: 1789, 1792–1797," Of Maps and Men, 2004, http:// libweb5.princeton.edu/visual_materials/maps/websites/northwest-passage/mackenzie.htm.

Chapter 10: Distracters

1. Colin Powell, "18 Lessons for Leaders," Ten3 Business e-Coach, www.1000ventures.com/business_guide/crosscuttings/leadership_ 18lessons_bycp.html.

2. Chuck Martin, "Hold That Thought!" Darwin: Information for Executives, October 24, 2005, www2.darwinmag.com/read/feature/ oct05_interrupt.cfm.

3. Os Guinness, *The Devil's Gauntlet* (Downer's Grove, IL: InterVarsity Press, 1989), www.bible.org/illus.php?topic_id=431.

4. J. M. Boice, *Nehemiah: Learning to Lead* (Grand Rapids: Revell, 1990), 38.

Chapter 11: Diverters

1. Marty Linsky and Ronald A. Heifetz, *Leadership on the Line* (Harvard Business School Press, 2002).

2. Marty Linsky, quoted in Martha Lagace, "Leadership in Real Life," *HBS Working Knowledge*, http://hbswk.hbs.edu/item.jhtml?id= 2952&t=moral_leadership.

3. "Why Is Religion So Important in Modern Political Matters?" News Batch, May 2005, www.newsbatch.com/religion.htm.

4. David Barton, "Church in the U.S. Capitol," Wallbuilders, 2003, www
.wallbuilders.com/resources/search/detail.php?ResourceID=123.

5. J. Stanley Oakes Jr., "Keeping the Faith," *National Review Online*, January 26, 2006, www.nationalreview.com/comment/oakes200601260819
.asp.

6. David Aikman, *Great Souls: Six Who Changed the Century* (Nashville: Word, 1998), 125.

Chapter 12: Doubters

1. Os Guinness, *In Two Minds* (Downer's Grove, IL: InterVarsity Press, 1976).

2. C. S. Lewis, *Mere Christianity* (New York: MacMillan, 1952), 123.

3. Thomas Cahill, *How the Irish Saved Civilization* (New York: Anchor Books, 1996), 113.

Chapter 14: Foot Draggers

1. Winston Churchill, "Their Finest Hour," The Churchill Centre, June 18, 1940, www.winstonchurchill.org/i4a/pages/index.cfm?pageid=418.

Chapter 15: Freeloaders

1. Christopher M. Avery, "Getting Unstuck: Dealing with Unmotivated Team Members, Part 2," 3M, www.3m.com/meetingnetwork/readingroom/meetingguide_getting_unstuck2.html.

2. Brian Ross, "From Cash to Yachts: Congressman's Bribe Menu," ABC News, February 27, 2006, http://abcnews.go.com/Politics/story?id=1667009&page=1.

3. Ibid.

4. Elisa Lipsky-Karasz, "Land of the Freeloaders," *New York Post*, April 17, 2005, www.goofigure.com/UserGoofigureDetail.asp?gooID=5312.

5. Lori Majewski, quoted in Elisa Lipsky-Karasz, "Land of the Freeloaders," *New York Post*, April 17, 2005, www.goofigure.com/UserGoofigureDetail.asp?gooID=5312.

6. Lipsky-Karasz, "Land of the Freeloaders."

7. John Warren Kindt, quoted in Bernard P. Horn, "Is There a Cure for America's Gambling Addiction?" PBS online, www.pbs.org/wgbh/pages/frontline/shows/gamble/procon/horn.html.

8. *Cato Handbook for Congress* (Washington: The Cato Institute), www
.cato.org/pubs/handbook/hb108/hb108-33.pdf#search=%22Cato%20
Institute%20taxpayer%20goodies%20defend%22.

9. Barbara Oakley, "It Takes Two to Tango," *New Forums Press* 1, no. 1 (2003): 19–28.

10. Avery, "Getting Unstuck."

11. "Greenspan Urges Future Social Security Cuts," *Associated Press*, February 25, 2004.

12. Ibid.

13. Oakley, "It Takes Two to Tango."

Chapter 16: Patronizers

1. William Hazlitt, "On the Spirit of Obligations," *New Monthly Magazine*, 1824, www.blupete.com/Literature/Essays/Hazlitt/SpiritObliga tions.htm#fn1.

2. William Hazlitt, "On the Disadvantages of Intellectual Superiority," *Table Talk: Essays on Men and Manners*, 1822, www.blupete.com/Litera ture/Essays/Hazlitt/TableTalk/Superiority.htm.

3. William Shakespeare, "The Life and Death of Richard the Second," The Complete Works of William Shakespeare, www-tech.mit .edu/Shakespeare/richardii/richardii.2.1.html.

4. John Potempa, "Readers Report," *Business Week Online*, July 15, 2002, www.businessweek.com/magazine/content/02_28/c3791027 .htm.

5. Jim Collins, *Good to Great* (New York: HarperCollins, 2001). See especially Collins's discussion of "Level 5 Leadership," pages 17–40.

6. Manuel Velasquez, "What Really Went Wrong With Enron? A Culture of Evil?" Santa Clara University, 2002, www.scu.edu/ethics/pub lications/ethicalperspectives/enronpanel.html.

7. Joseph L. Ellis, *His Excellency George Washington* (New York: Random House, 2004), 147.

8. James H. Hutson, "John Adams' Title Campaign," *New England Quarterly* 41, no. 1 (1968): 30–39.

9. Jim Nelson Black, *When Nations Die* (Wheaton: Tyndale, 1994), 67.

10. Warren Bennis, quoted in Ira Chaleff, "Leader-Follower Dynamics," *Innovative Leader*, August 2003, www.winstonbrill.com/bril001/ html/article_index/articles/551-600/article582_body.html.

11. "Good Put-Downs," H2G2, August 9, 2002, www.bbc.co.uk/dna/ h2g2/A765876.

Chapter 17: Pot Stirrers

1. Paul Kenneth Glass, "Manage Your Destructive Employees," *Psychology for Business* 3, no. 5 (2002), www.psychologyforbusiness.com/ DestructiveEmployees.htm.

2. Noel M. Tichy and Mary Anne Devanna, *The Transformational Leader* (New York: John Wiley & Sons, 1990), 221.

3. "Taming the Fires of Employee Conflict," Ceridian Connection, January 2005, www.ceridian.com/myceridian/connection/article/archive/0,3263,12437-56654,00.html.

4. Charles E. Reed, "Written Statement of Charles E. Reed, M.D., Before the United States House of Representatives' Subcommittee on Oversight and Investigations, Committee on Education and the Workforce," March 25, 1999, http://commdocs.house.gov/committees/edu/hedo&i6-16.000/hedo&i6-16.htm.

5. Ibid.

6. Johannes P. Louw and Eugene A. Nida, *Greek-English Lexicon Based on Semantic Domains* (New York: United Bible Societies, 1988). Used by permission.

7. Rod Walsh and Dan Carrison, "Reassuring Employees After Layoffs," Entrepreneur.com, September 17, 2001, www.entrepreneur.com/article/0,4621,292949,00.html.

8. Ibid.

9. Ibid.

10. Glass, "Manage Your Destructive Employees."

Chapter 18: Quitters

1. Gregory P. Smith, "Top Ten Reasons Why People Quit Their Jobs," The CEO Refresher, 2002, www.refresher.com/!gpsquit.html.

2. "Bits & Pieces," Bible.org, www.bible.org/bits/toc.htm.

3. Ibid.

4. Ibid.

5. Noel M. Tichy, *Managing Strategic Change* (New York: John Wiley & Sons, 1983), 332.

6. Ibid.

7. Edgar H. Schein, *Organizational Culture and Leadership* (San Francisco: Jossey-Bass, 1992), 127–30.

8. Jack Fitzenz, quoted in Jim Harris and Joan Brannick, *Finding & Keeping Great Employees* (New York: American Management Association, 1999), 12.

9. Smith, "Top Ten Reasons Why People Quit Their Jobs."

10. Edward Morris, "A Revolutionary Idea," First Person BookPage, 2005, www.bookpage.com/0506bp/david_mccullough.html.

11. Gary Inrig, *A Call to Excellence* (Wheaton: Victor Books, 1985), 62.

12. Rich Lamb, "Burned Out? Could Be Your Attitude . . ." InterVarsity Student Leadership, 1999, www.intervarsity.org/slj/fa99/fa99_ll_burned_out_attitude.html.

13. Robert Jensen, "Why I Am a Christian (Sort Of)," AlterNet, March 10, 2006, www.alternet.org/story/33236/.

14. Ralph Waldo Emerson, quoted in Peggy Noonan, *When Character Was King* (New York: Viking, 2001), frontispiece.

Chapter 19: Stride Breakers

1. Craig Brian Larson, "Strong to the Finish," Christianity Today International, www.preachingtodaysermons.com/larcraigbria.html.

2. Rudolph W. Giuliani with Ken Kurson, *Leadership* (New York: Hyperion, 2002), 380.

3. Ibid., 108.

4. Collins, *Good to Great*, 206.

Chapter 20: Whiners

1. JoAnna Brandi, "Creating a Positive Employee Attitude in the Workplace," The Sideroad, 2006, www.sideroad.com/Management/employee_attitude.html.

2. Michelle Malkin, "Hard Labor, Soft Laborers," *Jewish World Review*, August 31, 2001, www.jewishworldreview.com/michelle/malkin083101.asp.

3. Danny Cox, *Leadership When the Heat's On*, 112.

4. Nancy Evans, "20 Ways to Deal with Difficult Co-Workers," iVillage, http://love.ivillage.com/fnf/fnfwork/0,,mxkw,00.html?arrival SA=1&cobrandRef=0&arrival_freqCap=2.

5. Brandi, "Creating a Positive Employee Attitude in the Workplace."

Chapter 21: Wounders

1. Thomas Blass, "The Man Who Shocked the World," *Psychology Today*, March/April 2002, www.psychologytoday.com/articles/pto-20020301-000037.html.

2. Hannah Arendt, quoted in Peter DeGratton, "An Extreme Example? Using Arendt's *Eichmann in Jerusalem* in the Business Ethics Classroom," *Essays in Philosophy*, June 2005, www.humboldt.edu/~essays/gatton.html.

3. Amy L. Aberg McLelland, "What Is the Taubman Approach?" Developing a Healthy Piano Technic, mclellandpiano.homestead.com/Preface.html.

4. John Pollock, *John Wesley, Servant of God* (Wheaton: Victor Books, 1989), 80.

5. Ibid.

6. Joseph J. Ellis, *His Excellency George Washington*, 129.

7. Ibid.

8. Ibid., 130.